PRESCRIPTIONS: THERAPEUTIC POEMS FOR THE IIEALING OF DEPRESSION

Dr. Perri Johnson

PRESS

Acknowledgements

This book has been a long time coming. I wish to dedicate this book to my mother, Dora Johnson, who died in 2002. She planted the seed that gave impetus to this writing. I thank my alter mother, Marietta Pinner, for watering the seed on a daily basis. I thank God for developing the seed into maturity over the past two years.

My special thanks go out to my children Kevin, Simone and Mareque who are a continual source of exhilaration. Great love and thanks to Tosucha Johnson who has contributed stupendously to my success. I thank my sister, Gwendolyn Dudley, for giving me input and love throughout the process. I thank Charlie and Sherri Johnson for their unwavering sense of family and friendship. I thank my aunt Lil for her love and thoughtfulness and my cousins Elizabeth and Tyrone Greene, James Coppedge, and Harold Coppedge for their love and support.

Heart-felt thanks go to radio personality, Mimi Brown, for friendship, prayers, and encouragement throughout the writing of this book. Sincere thanks to Suzanne Lopez for her counseling and coaching. Thanks to Dr. Patricia Johnson for her support and help. Thanks to Dr. Gail Jackson for her friendship and interest. Professional thanks to Michel Jean Phillippe for photography and Dr. Tim Gust for research.

I thank my family at In His Presence Church for lifting me up 24-7. Special thanks go to prayer warriors Rachel Oden, Arleen Milian, Christopher Johnson, Chris Hayes, and Luis Lopez.

I thank Zussette Pate for her enthusiasm, excitement, and right-hand help in accomplishing this work. Thanks to Monica Chamberlin for her dedication and assistantship. Not to be forgotten for their support are Andrea Evans, Lorena Vasquez, Pearline Railey-Neal, and Rebecca Reyna.

Gratefulness is extended to my mom and dad who continue to live within me. Much love is extended to my brother Andrew and sisters Delores and Edith. Bountiful thanks go to god-parents, Eugene and Louise Cofield.

In Memory of Skeets McClain.

Table of Contents

Introduction... *ix*
How to Use this Book.. *xi*
Formulary for Depressive...*xv*
Prelude... *xxix*

Chapter One
    Defining Depression...33
Chapter Two
    The Course of Depression..39
Chapter Three
    Depressive Thinking Styles...47
Chapter Four
    Conditions and Events Associated with
        Depression...51
        Loneliness..51
        Loss...56
        Grieving and Mourning..59
        Suicidal Ideations and Behaviors...................62
Chapter Five
    Coping with Depression..71
Chapter Six
    Treatment of Depression..81
        Cognitive-Behavioral Therapy Interventions......81
        Challenging Maladaptive Thinking.....................88

Adjusting Distorted Thinking *91*
Cognitive Restructuring *98*
Overcoming Childhood Programming *101*
Thought Stopping *104*
Reality Testing *106*
Detoxification *109*
Activity Scheduling *112*
Exercise *119*
Altruistic Activity *121*
Sleep Hygiene *124*
Positive Psychology *128*
Prayer *128*
Journaling *131*
Chapter Seven
   Depression Inoculation Strategies *135*
     Embracing the Experience *135*
       Acceptance *138*
       Regaining One's Power *140*
Chapter Eight
   Relapse Prevention *145*
     Embracing the Now *149*
     Ounce of Prevention *152*
     Observing Warning Signs *155*
Chapter Nine
   The Power of Optimism *159*

Introduction

This book is written especially for those who are in the midst of a depressive episode. It is intended to provide the essential knowledge, tools, and understanding to overcome the pain and distress associated with depression. This work is also written for people who are vulnerable to the recurrence of a depressive episode, have vivid and ongoing memories of prior hurt and disappointment, relate well to periods of chronic emotional suffering, and experience recurring negative thoughts that stifle optimism. Additionally, the book is designed to be an aid to family, friends, and professionals who are looking for a novel approach to help people that suffer from depression connect with the body of knowledge well established to assist in helping them to better cope with and overcome their illness.

The symptoms, conditions, and circumstances covered in the succeeding chapters are conceptualized primarily from the orientation of cognitive-behavioral psychotherapy. However, there is an incorporation of positive psychology and Christian-based spirituality throughout the work to address the frequent need for interventions beyond the scope of the cognitive-behavioral approach.

Several years ago, I began to think about the use of poems to provide creative expression to psychological phenomena I found interesting. As I began the process, I soon realized the potential of poetry as a tool to capsulate therapeutic principles and practices, and render them effective to persons with diminished cognitive capacity as a result of depression. Poetry allows the therapeutic message to be succinct and memorable. People suffering from depression do not frequently have the resolve to labor through reading about or listening to the extensive information proven successful in degrading the experience of depression. Poems afford a format to allow therapeutic information to be concisely communicated with impact, emphasizing the bullets essential to understand and operationalize the beliefs and actions necessary to overcome a very debilitating disorder. In addition, poems, if liked, are readily memorized and can thus become a part of the mental repertoire that contradicts and thwarts self derogation, distorted thinking, and other maladaptive cognitions and behaviors.

The poems presented here will prove beneficial in positively affecting the broken spirit and uplifting the degenerated mind. The accompanying text will provide a lay, but clinical-based understanding of the processes involved in the precipitation and subsequent amelioration of depression.

How to Use This Book

⌘

Depression is often a very severe illness that can bring one to the brink of wanting to give up on life. It is a time when pain and discouragement are so intense that a promise of future happiness and pleasurable occurrences is beyond consideration. Troubling occurrences may be more effectively handled if they can be lumped into categories or thematic issues. In this manner, they can be systematically targeted for relief. The key is to consistently apply the therapeutic tools and resources found in this work to aggressively advance the fight against depression on a daily basis. It is hoped that the poems and literature found here will provide a source of healing and relief through increased understanding of the processes of depression—both in rhyme and in reason.

Prescriptions: Therapeutic Poems for the Healing of Depression is a combination of contemporary writing about depression and includes poems based on theory, research, and clinical practice that offer relief and inspiration to those suffering from acute and chronic depression across varying degrees of severity. *Each poem* attempts to relate to a common experience of depression and suggests strategies and behaviors to better handle or overcome the enormous affliction to well being. The poems are prescriptive for various types of depressive episodes. Each offers comfort through identification and inspiration by following the positive suggestions and internalizing the messages of hope nestled within. Many of these poems are to be read or memorized as daily affirmations.

Each poem is introduced by prose that describes corresponding clinical aspects of depression and implications for increased wellness through the understanding and self-help practices. The poems acknowledge the overwhelming challenges of coping with circumstances that exhaust the ordinary availability of personal resources. Each point to well-established therapeutic techniques and strategies used in cognitive-behavioral and positive psychology approaches to overcoming episodes of clinical depression.

The poems crystallize the concepts and practices necessary to decrease the intensity of suffering as well as the loss of social and occupational functioning. They are intended to be a source of inspiration, hope, instruction and optimism. *Use the poems to refute negative thinking and defend against esteem debasing indictments.*

Some of the poems draw upon the principles and teachings of Christ. Each recognizes that today marks a dark phase of a journey toward a brighter tomorrow. The most powerful poems offer an affirmation of what is expected to occur that does not presently exist. Subjects covered include loneliness, rejection, hopelessness, loss, feelings of inadequacy, anger, disappointment, suicidal thinking and behavior, confusion, prolonged unhappiness, self-pity, and other anomalies typical of depressed states that require treatment.

The information covered describes incidences, quality and intensity of characteristics, and provides insight into what creates and sustains depressive thoughts and emotions. It is useful for those actually suffering, as well as those attempting to help persons suffering with depression. The book may be read straight through to gain broad-based understanding with referenced concepts, or can be searched to locate poems with specific therapeutic qualities using the prescriptive formulary following this section. It is recommended that the book is read straight through and then researched for poems that apply to conditions and themes of suffering.

The formulary following this section cites conditions and circumstances that cause despair and prescriptively suggests poems that offer insight and provide therapeutic direction that essentially promotes healing.

Formulary for Depressive Conditions

❧

Apathy:

STUCK IN DEPRESSION...38

WOE IS ME...50

MUSING OF THE MIND...90

THE ONE WHO ENDURES...78

DON'T BRAIN STORM ALONE...84

DON'T SURRENDER THE MIND...105

LIFE'S PUZZLE...139

WHAT AM I? CHOPPED LIVER? (ON BEING ASSERTIVE)...143

THE TIDE WILL TURN...162

MY PLAN SAYS I CAN...165

Acutely Depressed:

STUCK IN DEPRESSION...38

TIME...42

WOE IS ME...50

MUSING OF THE MIND...90

SUICIDE...64

THE CONTINUUM...74

THE ONE WHO ENDURES...78

DON'T BRAIN STORM ALONE...84

THE MIND CAN OVERRULE THE MOOD...86

MUSING OF THE MIND...90
IT'S NOT ALL ON YOU...93
MOODS ARE SUBJECT TO THOUGHTS...100
DON'T SURRENDER THE MIND...105
DENIAL...108
GETTING PHYSICAL...120
ALTRUISTIC ACTIVITY: A QUICK FIX...123
REST...126
THE VALUE OF PAIN...137
LIFE'S PUZZLE...139
RAINY DAY MEMORIES...154
THE TIDE WILL TURN...162
MY PLAN SAYS I CAN...165

Break Up:

I WILL BE HAPPY AGAIN...xxxi
LONELINESS CONDITION...54
THE CONTINUUM...74
IT'S NOT ALL ON YOU...93
DENIAL...108
A RIDDLE...111
ALTRUISTIC ACTIVITY: A QUICK FIX...123
LIFE'S PUZZLE...139
WHAT AM I? CHOPPED LIVER? (ON BEING ASSERTIVE)...143
RAINY DAY MEMORIES...154
THE TIDE WILL TURN...162

Confused Mind:

TIME...42
MUSING OF THE MIND...90
DON'T BRAIN STORM ALONE...89
THE MIND CAN OVERRULE THE MOOD...86
ISSUES: DOWN HOME BLUES...103
DON'T SURRENDER THE MIND...105
DENIAL...108

GETTING PHYSICAL...120
REST...126
LIFE'S PUZZLE...139
DRIVE DEFENSIVELY (SORROW PREVENTION)...157
THE TIDE WILL TURN...162
MY PLAN SAYS I CAN...165

Chronic Depression:

STUCK IN DEPRESSION...38
A COURSE OF EVENTS...45
WOE IS ME...50
MUSING OF THE MIND...90
SUICIDE...64
THE CONTINUUM...74
THE ONE WHO ENDURES...78
DON'T BRAIN STORM ALONE...84
THE MIND CAN OVERRULE THE MOOD...86
IT'S NOT ALL ON YOU...93
MOODS ARE SUBJECT TO THOUGHTS...100
DON'T SURRENDER THE MIND...105
DENIAL...108
ACTIVITY: A NECESSARY CONDITION...114
CAN I?...117
GETTING PHYSICAL...120
ALTRUISTIC ACTIVITY: A QUICK FIX...123
REST...126
RAINY DAY MEMORIES...154
THE TIDE WILL TURN...162
MY PLAN SAYS I CAN 165

Denial:

DENIAL...108
THE VALUE OF PAIN...137
WHAT AM I? CHOPPED LIVER? (ON BEING ASSERTIVE)...143
DRIVE DEFENSIVELY (SORROW PREVENTION)...157

Dejection:

I WILL BE HAPPY AGAIN...xxxi
TIME...42
A COURSE OF EVENTS...45
WOE IS ME...50
MUSING OF THE MIND...90
THE CONTINUUM...74
THE ONE WHO ENDURES...78
DON'T BRAIN STORM ALONE...84
THE MIND CAN OVERRULE THE MOOD...86
MOODS ARE SUBJECT TO THOUGHTS...100
DON'T SURRENDER THE MIND...105
ALTRUISTIC ACTIVITY: A QUICK FIX...123
THE VALUE OF PAIN...137
PERSONAL CONTROL...148
THE FUTURE IS NOW...151
RAINY DAY MEMORIES...154
THE TIDE WILL TURN...162
MY PLAN SAYS I CAN...165

Disappointment in Love Life

I WILL BE HAPPY AGAIN...xxxi
TIME...42
WOE IS ME...50
MUSING OF THE MIND...90
LONELINESS CONDITION...54
THE CONTINUUM...74
THE ONE WHO ENDURES...78
DON'T BRAIN STORM ALONE...84
IT'S NOT ALL ON YOU...93
DON'T SURRENDER THE MIND...105
A RIDDLE...111
LIFE'S PUZZLE...139
WHAT AM I? CHOPPED LIVER? (ON BEING ASSERTIVE)...143
PERSONAL CONTROL...148

THE FUTURE IS NOW...151
RAINY DAY MEMORIES...154
THE TIDE WILL TURN...162

Discouragement:

I WILL BE HAPPY AGAIN...xxxi
TIME...42
A COURSE OF EVENTS...45
WOE IS ME...50
MUSING OF THE MIND...90
SUICIDE...64
THE CONTINUUM...74
THE ONE WHO ENDURES...78
DON'T BRAIN STORM ALONE...84
THE MIND CAN OVERRULE THE MOOD...86
MUSING OF THE MIND...90
MOODS ARE SUBJECT TO THOUGHTS...100
DON'T SURRENDER THE MIND...105
REST...126
THE VALUE OF PAIN...137
LIFE'S PUZZLE...139
THE FUTURE IS NOW...151
RAINY DAY MEMORIES...154
THE TIDE WILL TURN...162
MY PLAN SAYS I CAN...165

Divorce:

I WILL BE HAPPY AGAIN...xxxi
LONELINESS CONDITION...54
THE CONTINUUM...74
IT'S NOT ALL ON YOU...93
DON'T SURRENDER THE MIND...105
DENIAL...108
A RIDDLE...111
ALTRUISTIC ACTIVITY: A QUICK FIX...123

LIFE'S PUZZLE...139
RAINY DAY MEMORIES...466
THE TIDE WILL TURN...162

Emotionally Wounded
I WILL BE HAPPY AGAIN...xxxi
STUCK IN DEPRESSION...38
A COURSE OF EVENTS...45
WOE IS ME...50
MUSING OF THE MIND...90
THE CONTINUUM...74
THE ONE WHO ENDURES...78
DON'T BRAIN STORM ALONE...84
THE MIND CAN OVERRULE THE MOOD...86
MUSING OF THE MIND...90
IT'S NOT ALL ON YOU...93
MOODS ARE SUBJECT TO THOUGHTS...100
ISSUES: DOWN HOME BLUES...103
DON'T SURRENDER THE MIND...105
A RIDDLE...111
CAN I?...117
ALTRUISTIC ACTIVITY: A QUICK FIX...123
THE VALUE OF PAIN...137
THE TIDE WILL TURN...162
MY PLAN SAYS I CAN...165

Family Childhood Dysfunction:
DON'T BRAIN STORM ALONE...84
ISSUES: DOWN HOME BLUES...103
A RIDDLE...111

Feeling Bummed Out:
BLUE ACHOO...35
MUSING OF THE MIND...90
THE CONTINUUM...74

THE MIND CAN OVERRULE THE MOOD...86
MOODS ARE SUBJECT TO THOUGHTS...100
DON'T SURRENDER THE MIND...105
GETTING PHYSICAL...120
REST...126
THE FUTURE IS NOW...151
RAINY DAY MEMORIES...154
THE TIDE WILL TURN...162

Frustration:

MUSING OF THE MIND...90
THE CONTINUUM...74
DON'T SURRENDER THE MIND...105
GETTING PHYSICAL...120
LIFE'S PUZZLE...139
WHAT AM I? CHOPPED LIVER? (ON BEING ASSERTIVE)...143
PERSONAL CONTROL...148
THE FUTURE IS NOW...151
RAINY DAY MEMORIES...154
DRIVE DEFENSIVELY (SORROW PREVENTION)...157
THE TIDE WILL TURN...162

Going Crazy:

STUCK IN DEPRESSION...38
MUSING OF THE MIND...90
THE CONTINUUM...74
SUICIDE...64
THE ONE WHO ENDURES...78
DON'T BRAIN STORM ALONE...84
THE MIND CAN OVERRULE THE MOOD...86
DON'T SURRENDER THE MIND...105
DENIAL...108
GETTING PHYSICAL...120
REST...126

THE TIDE WILL TURN...162
MY PLAN SAYS I CAN...165

Grieving:

REMEMBERING...58
YOU'RE GONE...WE'RE HERE...68
THE ONE WHO ENDURES...78
DON'T BRAIN STORM ALONE...84
DON'T SURRENDER THE MIND...105
DENIAL...108
CAN I?...117
RAINY DAY MEMORIES...154
MY PLAN SAYS I CAN...165

Hopelessness:

STUCK IN DEPRESSION...38
A COURSE OF EVENTS...45
WOE IS ME...50
SUICIDE...64
THE CONTINUUM...74
THE ONE WHO ENDURES...78
DON'T BRAIN STORM ALONE...84
THE MIND CAN OVERRULE THE MOOD...86
DON'T SURRENDER THE MIND...105
CAN I?...117
RAINY DAY MEMORIES...154
THE TIDE WILL TURN...162
MY PLAN SAYS I CAN...165

Hurting:

I WILL BE HAPPY AGAIN...xxxi
TIME...42
LONELINESS CONDITION...54
THE CONTINUUM...74
THE ONE WHO ENDURES...78

THE MIND CAN OVERRULE THE MOOD...86
DENIAL...108
A RIDDLE...111
ACTIVITY: A NECESSARY CONDITION...114
CAN I?...117
ALTRUISTIC ACTIVITY: A QUICK FIX...123
THE VALUE OF PAIN...137
LIFE'S PUZZLE...139
RAINY DAY MEMORIES...154
DRIVE DEFENSIVELY (SORROW PREVENTION)...157
THE TIDE WILL TURN...162
MY PLAN SAYS I CAN...165

Isolation and Withdrawal:

STUCK IN DEPRESSION...38
A COURSE OF EVENTS...45
WOE IS ME...50
LONELINESS CONDITION...54
SUICIDE...64
THE ONE WHO ENDURES...78
DON'T BRAIN STORM ALONE...84
THE MIND CAN OVERRULE THE MOOD...86
DON'T SURRENDER THE MIND...105
ACTIVITY: A NECESSARY CONDITION...114
CAN I?...117
GETTING PHYSICAL...120
RAINY DAY MEMORIES...154
THE TIDE WILL TURN...162

Loneliness:

I WILL BE HAPPY AGAIN...xxxi
LONELINESS CONDITION...54
THE CONTINUUM...74
DON'T SURRENDER THE MIND...105
ACTIVITY: A NECESSARY CONDITION...114

GETTING PHYSICAL...120
THE FUTURE IS NOW...151
RAINY DAY MEMORIES...154
THE TIDE WILL TURN...162
LIFE AFTER LOSS...61
DENIAL...108
RAINY DAY MEMORIES...154

Mourning:

REMEMBERING...58
LIFE AFTER LOSS...61
RAINY DAY MEMORIES...154

Negativism:

THE CONTINUUM...74
THE ONE WHO ENDURES...78
THE MIND CAN OVERRULE THE MOOD...86
MUSING OF THE MIND...90
MOODS ARE SUBJECT TO THOUGHTS...100
ISSUES: DOWN HOME BLUES...111
THE VALUE OF PAIN...137
PERSONAL CONTROL...148
THE FUTURE IS NOW...151
RAINY DAY MEMORIES...154
DRIVE DEFENSIVELY (SORROW PREVENTION)...157
THE TIDE WILL TURN...162

Overwhelmed:

MUSING OF THE MIND...90
SUICIDE...64
THE CONTINUUM...74
THE ONE WHO ENDURES...78
DON'T BRAIN STORM ALONE...89
THE MIND CAN OVERRULE THE MOOD...86
MUSING OF THE MIND...90

DON'T SURRENDER THE MIND...105
GETTING PHYSICAL...120
REST...126
LIFE'S PUZZLE...139
DRIVE DEFENSIVELY (SORROW PREVENTION)...157
THE TIDE WILL TURN...162
MY PLAN SAYS I CAN...165

Rejection:

MUSING OF THE MIND...90
THE ONE WHO ENDURES...78
DON'T BRAIN STORM ALONE...84
DON'T SURRENDER THE MIND...105
DENIAL...108
THE VALUE OF PAIN...137
LIFE'S PUZZLE...139
WHAT AM I? CHOPPED LIVER? (ON BEING ASSERTIVE)...143
PERSONAL CONTROL...148
THE TIDE WILL TURN...162

Relationship Demise:

I WILL BE HAPPY AGAIN...xxxi
THE CONTINUUM...74
MUSING OF THE MIND...90
LONELINESS CONDITION...54
THE ONE WHO ENDURES...78
DON'T BRAIN STORM ALONE...84
THE MIND CAN OVERRULE THE MOOD...86
MUSING OF THE MIND 90
IT'S NOT ALL ON YOU...93
DON'T SURRENDER THE MIND...105
DENIAL...108
A RIDDLE...111
ALTRUISTIC ACTIVITY: A QUICK FIX...123
THE VALUE OF PAIN...137

LIFE'S PUZZLE...139
WHAT AM I? CHOPPED LIVER? (ON BEING ASSERTIVE)...143
THE TIDE WILL TURN...162

Severe Depression:
WOE IS ME...50
STUCK IN DEPRESSION...38
SUICIDE...64
THE CONTINUUM...74
THE ONE WHO ENDURES...78
DON'T BRAIN STORM ALONE...84
THE MIND CAN OVERRULE THE MOOD...86
IT'S NOT ALL ON YOU...93
MOODS ARE SUBJECT TO THOUGHTS...100
DON'T SURRENDER THE MIND...105
DENIAL...108
ACTIVITY: A NECESSARY CONDITION...114
CAN I?...117
GETTING PHYSICAL...120
ALTRUISTIC ACTIVITY: A QUICK FIX...123
REST...126
THE VALUE OF PAIN...137
WHAT AM I? CHOPPED LIVER? (ON BEING ASSERTIVE)...143
THE TIDE WILL TURN...162
MY PLAN SAYS I CAN...165

Stagnation/Desolation, Self -neglect:
STUCK IN DEPRESSION...38
A COURSE OF EVENTS...45
WOE IS ME...50
SUICIDE...64
DON'T BRAIN STORM ALONE...84
THE MIND CAN OVERRULE THE MOOD...86
DON'T SURRENDER THE MIND...105
ACTIVITY: A NECESSARY CONDITION...114

CAN I?...117
GETTING PHYSICAL...120
THE TIDE WILL TURN...162

Sorrowful Circumstances:

TIME...42
WOE IS ME...50
A COURSE OF EVENTS...45
MUSING OF THE MIND...90
SUICIDE...64
THE CONTINUUM...74
THE ONE WHO ENDURES...78
DON'T BRAIN STORM ALONE...84
IT'S NOT ALL ON YOU...93
MOODS ARE SUBJECT TO THOUGHTS...100
DON'T SURRENDER THE MIND...105
DENIAL...108
GETTING PHYSICAL...120
THE VALUE OF PAIN...137
LIFE'S PUZZLE...139
RAINY DAY MEMORIES...154
THE TIDE WILL TURN...162

Starting Over Again:

LONELINESS CONDITION...54
THE CONTINUUM...74
A RIDDLE...111
ACTIVITY: A NECESSARY CONDITION...114
CAN I?...117
WHAT AM I? CHOPPED LIVER? (ON BEING ASSERTIVE)...143
THE FUTURE IS NOW...151
DRIVE DEFENSIVELY (SORROW PREVENTION)...157
THE TIDE WILL TURN...162
MY PLAN SAYS I CAN...165

Suicidal:

STUCK IN DEPRESSION...38
WOE IS ME...50
MUSING OF THE MIND...90
SUICIDAL...68
YOU'RE GONE...WE'RE HERE...68
THE CONTINUUM...74
THE ONE WHO ENDURES...78
DON'T BRAIN STORM ALONE...84
THE MIND CAN OVERRULE THE MOOD...86
IT'S NOT ALL ON YOU...93
DON'T SURRENDER THE MIND...105
REST...126
THE VALUE OF PAIN...137
THE TIDE WILL TURN...162
MY PLAN SAYS I CAN...165

Prelude

❧

Fundamental to our ability to thrive is a sense of optimism. It inspires hope. It is an elixir that promotes vigor to endure depressing conditions. An affirmation of optimism goes a long way to encourage inspiration from a sunken state of despair. Optimism breeds confidence. Confidence propels a person to continue in positive effort to overcome formidable obstacles. In essence, this persistence provides the study grind that eventually cracks the rock (Carver and Scheier, 2005). Most assuredly, there can be no true victory without a fight. Optimism is a therapeutic antagonist that opposes the negative thoughts and bad feelings that depression can cause.

The potency of optimism as an ameliorative agent is foundational to this book; therefore, it is continually restated throughout the prose and poetry in this work. It encourages one who is suffering with despair and discouragement to remain hopeful, and more importantly to look for the rainbow at the end of the storm. It emphasizes the temporariness of the adverse circumstances and promotes an active "willingness" for conditions to change. Optimism supports religious faith. Likewise, the placebo effect and basic tenants of quantum physics postulate a positive correlation between targeted outcomes and corresponding beliefs in their future manifestations.

Before we begin to explore the wide range of causes, symptoms, and implications of depression and its antidotes, I introduce this first poem to underscore the importance of optimism. It verses a mantra of determination to replace today's sorrow with the joys of tomorrow's unfolding. Recited daily, this poem speaks to the heart to cause encouragement. This is an essential element in overcoming the despair associated with depression.

Prescription: Read or recite the entire poem daily upon getting started. Throughout the day, repeat the refrain, especially when disparaging thoughts and feelings become pronounced. Continue this schedule for three to six months, and then as needed.

I Will Be Happy Again

Eventually the river of tears will end
I will be happy again.
Time is the variable between now and then
I will be happy again.
Winter solstice comes before spring can begin
I will be happy again.
History shows a continuous change in trend
I will be happy again.
As the world turns a heart will mend
I will be happy again.
I will let go of "how did this happen?"
I will be happy again.
I will get up from where I've fallen
I will be happy again.

Chapter One

Defining Depression

Ordinary Depression

Despite the abundance of good information available that describes depression, many people are confused about what depression is and what it is not. This is perhaps for very good reason. Almost everyone goes through a period of depression. Surely we all experience a series of bad events, disappointments, setbacks, emotional confusion, psychological despair, and just some plain old drama. There is a great distinction between the "down in the dumps" that affects most people at least once a year and that described by the definition of clinical depression. The major distinction between the kind of depression common to all and clinical depression is the severity and duration of symptoms, and its decisive impact on day-to-day functioning (American Psychiatric Association [APA], 2000). Fortunately, or unfortunately (depending on the way you look at it), we all experience events that really wear us down. Surely, everyone has episodes of downs that cause disappointment and unhappiness. Bouts of depressive feelings, sadness, brooding and disappointment that do not persist for an extended period, allow almost normal day-to-day functioning to occur, dampen the experience of life but do not sap the energy and optimism that is characteristic of effective coping with adversity represent instances of challenges that are like minor storms in life. These are times when we say, "I'm depressed" and do not mean to communicate anything that is of dire consequence. Perhaps, this is why many people have a hard time showing empathy for persons going through clinical depression. They may find it difficult to make a distinction between the less severe and very transient state of depressed feelings common to everyone from time to time. *The range of distance between the major depressive episode and a state of blues is similar to the difference between the serious and potentially life threatening case of pneumonia and the flu. The latter runs an uncomfortable but readily manageable, short-lived course of illness. It's a pain, but does not cause the havoc characteristic of a clinical encounter.*

The next poem makes a distinction between the kind of common depressed state that has parity with a common cold and that of a much more serious, if not crippling nature. The common case slows progress and adversely impacts day-to-day quality of life for a rather short duration. It describes a benign condition that should be answered with a "rest and chicken soup" approach. Like any attack on the human organism, it is best to address distressful conditions that are not major before they evolve into more serious conditions.

Prescription: This poem is a prescription for subclinical depression. Read this poem once per day when you feel bummed out. The poem targets a time of psychological impact, but relates to an emotional state that is not severely and persistently disordered.

Blue Achoo

Sometimes we'll be blue for a day or two
Or three or four or maybe a little more
Just like the physical self
The emotional being lapses in health
Things so stressful that it wears us down
A circumstance so vexing that it draws a frown
Makes us want to quit and throw in the towel
Angers us to scream, rant and rave and howl
The blahs may alter our ways for several days

We rest, adjust, and rebound to once again hit the
ground
We do not allow the germinating to persist
We build up, fight back, and resist
It's an emotional flu
A bug that bites you
Menaces and then it's through
We're all susceptible to
A blue achoo

Clinical Depression

Although the condition described in the preceding section can represent a challenge to peace of mind and productive activity, it does not impact the Richter scale as an episode of clinical depression registers. *A major depressive episode is evidenced by a period of two weeks or more of pronounced sadness or despondency that does not remit the entire day, almost every day of the week. There are usually dramatic changes in sleeping and eating patterns that may increase or decrease. There can be an actual slowing of movement, as well as impairment in concentration, memory, and decision making. Frequently, there is a sustained loss of pleasure, fatigue, and lack of purpose, often accompanied by feelings of worthlessness and hopelessness.* When severe, persons may have thoughts of death or develop ideas and intentions of committing suicide (APA, 2000). This caliber of depression is referred to as *Clinical Depression*. The major depressive episode affects a large percentage of the population.

About 20 percent of the American population will suffer an episode of clinical depression (Gotlib and Hammen, 2002). Not infrequently, the best efforts and support from others are not sufficient to remedy the intense pain and sorrow. When the depressive storm is of this magnitude, there may be a strong sense of futility. This is especially true when week after week the overwhelming feelings of personal tragedy, emptiness, and lack of ability to find adequate solutions persist. It is at this time that the person suffering should seek professional help and treatment. Many people are reluctant to seek professional help despite the astounding fact that depression is very treatable. Most disheartening is the statistic that suggests approximately 15 percent of the depressed population will commit suicide.

Women represent the largest segment of the depressed population (Gotlib and Hammen, 2002). However, approximately 40 percent of women do not seek help for depression for various psycho-social reasons, one of which is embarrassment. Reluctance to seek treatment is astounding in many minority populations. For example, 98 percent of depressed African American men do not seek treatment. This is tragic given the established effectiveness of cognitive behavioral therapy, medications, or a combination of both in treating depression.

If a depressive episode persists beyond two weeks and self-help measures do not prove effective, professional help should be sought and treatment strategies developed. It is important to not remain immersed in depression.

The next poem describes the degree of agony a person suffering with clinical depression may experience during an episode. It depicts the kind of condition that is not readily overcome without psychotherapy or counseling. This poem is to be read by or shared with persons experiencing pronounced symptoms of clinical depression and not yet committed to treatment. It is hoped that by relating to these feelings and symptoms, he or she will come to the realization that professional help is needed.

Prescription: For acute depression. Recite three times daily, preferably morning, afternoon, and before bed. Continue until engaged in therapy and severe despair has lifted.

Stuck In Depression

Spinning wheels, not moving ahead
The more I look the less I see
Sometimes thinking I'd be better off dead
The answers to my problems just seem to elude me

Difficult to cope with such trying times
Often more than I feel I can take
Hard to ignore the warning signs
I'm at a loss for what turns to make

Night and day I can't escape
Surges of sadness flooding my panes
Darkness hung from the clouds to drape
Unfathomable perplexity to drive me insane

No desires or interests that peak
Feeling incompetent to face the fears
Appetite gone, can't get no sleep
Drowning my problems in whiskey and beers

Short of mind to manage my affairs
Blaming myself for things going south
Questioning whether anybody really cares
Would ask, but words are hard to mouth

In need of help, can't find a source
Haunting thoughts that end this misery
Each day feeling deep remorse

Truth is, I need therapy

Chapter Two

The course of Depression

❦

How Long Will It Last?

The essence of clinical depression is an intense feeling of dissatisfaction with oneself, circumstances, and hopes for the future. It is an intense sadness and discouragement that overwhelms the ordinary capacity to shrug it off. In fact, despite the best efforts to come out of feeling down in the dumps, the mood remains pronounced. It is difficult to avoid showing the appearance of not coping well with the present unfortunate life event. Often, it is difficult to find pleasure in activities or relationships that had previously been sources of pleasure. Also, as mentioned earlier, *a clinical or major depressive episode generally compromises many cognitive and behavioral functions including the ability to sleep well, concentrate, and make decisions. It often surfaces feelings of guilt, worthlessness, and inadequacy. Frequently, it takes away the desire and energy to get out of bed and face the world* (APA, 2000). Importantly, *the depressed person perceives these distraught feelings and behavioral disturbances as never ending.*

The concept that the signs and symptoms of depression are transient is one of several recurrent themes running throughout the poetry and prose. The temporariness of the suffering condition is heavily emphasized because the depressed person frequently loses contact with reality of the inevitability of change, especially as it pertains to an improvement of the current, dreadful circumstances. There is an overwhelming tendency to perceive the affliction as pervasive and unyielding. If the instability of the dark, sorrowful mood can be realized, then the promise of feeling better can be more quickly brought into the realm of possibility. It is often quite difficult to see the time limited existence of the malignant circumstances. There may be an austere pessimism about the future that undermines the sense of patience necessary to wait on the upturn of events. Awareness of the temporary nature of the suffering enables one to tolerate the conditions until change occurs. The essential capacities needed here are patience and endurance. Most often, these are qualities unavailable to the depressed person. However, if the depressed person can be assisted to see and appreciate the potential for dramatic change in a finite matter of time, he or she is less likely to fall victim to a sense of unrelenting futility and doom.

The next poem is philosophical. It depicts a sequence of occurrences that follow a succinct flow toward resolution over time. The problem is that the anguish resulting from those conditions begging for resolution is so intense that it generates a great sense of urgency to find immediate answers and care. Indeed, it is here that the wisdom talked about in the Serenity Prayer comes in. There are some things we are powerless to change. Moreover, some things require a level of understanding beyond what is currently available to bring about meaningful, positive change. To that end, energy invested in exercising the patience to allow the time to give additional pieces of the puzzle to make the developing picture clear is far more productive than the spinning of wheels and going nowhere, spoken of in the previous poem (*Stuck in Depression*).

Prescription: Read the following poem each morning to establish and reinforce a mind set of looking at increments of time to bring about the understanding and constitution needed to temper the adversity of the existing grave circumstances. The poem serves as a good theme for daily meditations.

Time

All mysteries will unravel in time
And confusion will be clarified
A future date is specified
To resolve what challenges the boggled mind

Time yields the paths of correction to choose
Raises the blinds so light can come in
Rings the alarm to come out of a snooze
Signals a new course of action to begin

Is appointed by a Godly plan
Works toward a purpose that envelops all
Gives seasons a course to span
A chance for people to evolve

Wait to take advantage of a new moment
Depression is but a section the pendulum swings
Melancholia is a temporary postponement
Of new life that the passage of time brings

This too shall pass

Overcoming depression requires coping strategies that allow a real-time understanding and response to the challenges presented by its symptoms with effective and encouraging thinking and behavior. Often, the feeling of overwhelming despair and pain nullifies the suggestions that the condition of suffering is temporary. *The sense that one cannot endure what seems to be an unrelenting course of disparagement is one of the most challenging aspects of coping with depression.* Without markers to signal progress, it is extremely difficult to envision an end to the misery, let alone a subsequent transition into an enhanced quality of life. It is this very stickler point that denies the mind the perspective that the depressive circumstances are fleeting. Since depression generally makes everyday living burdensome, the continuation of the circumstances over an extended period makes life very discouraging. As a consequence, it becomes more and more challenging to realize the temporariness of a depressive episode. *The experience of clinical depression feels never ending. It hovers like a persisting, dreadful now.* This perception begs to be persuaded differently.

The notion of temporariness can be a difficult concept to embrace when there are no apparent measures of progress being made. When talking to depressed clients during the initial stages of treatment of depression, I can readily see the disbelief that surfaces upon the suggestion that the dread and sorrowfulness presently experienced will generally pass in a matter of months. *Depression, like most problems, is very susceptible to coercion to end given time and effort.* The benefit of therapy is that the therapist helps the person suffering to realize markers that indicate progress. Once incremental progress is noted, an anticipation of future progress can be hoped for. *As optimism is increased and evidence of positive change is realized, the signs and symp-*

toms of depression are attenuated. If the suffering person can be assisted to maintain a strategy that promotes ongoing determination, a positive feedback loop can be established to show that progress toward resolution is, in fact, being made. Subsequently, the obstacles encountered will not readily discourage the commitment to endure until a positive outcome is achieved.

Inspiration from depression's doldrums is buoyed by an understanding of the process of change, sustained effort, and optimism. The next poem describes the process of going through a depressive episode. It walks one through the phases and shows light at the end of the tunnel. It speaks of a finite span of time that encapsulates disparaging circumstances. It helps one to track the progression of change leading toward a state of resiliency.

Prescription: This poem is to be read weekly during the course of a depressive episode. It is food for thought that helps to inoculate against the exaggerated suffering that comes as a result of not knowing what to expect. Use this poem to self-encourage by talking oneself through the process of overcoming a bout of depression.

Depression: A Course of Events

Depression is the experience of time
Time that appears slowed
Painfully disturbing circumstances seem prolonged
Know that it is but for a fixed course of events
It is an intense but temporary condition
It passes
Surely, by increments
The duration is relative to severity and interventions
Prayer, professional treatment, and support help
A date on the calendar celebrates its end

The first days after reality sets in are dreadful
It worsens and feels unbearable
No end in sight
A dark tunnel
Darker and darker
Then... look... a flicker of light
Midway

A ray of hope
An encouraging sign
Indications of season change coming
Sunshine mixed with rain
Months gone by
Bumps but no potholes in the road

Dawning of new days
Awareness of faces and possibilities
Smiles and laughter on occasions
Time says enough is enough
Depression lifts

Chapter Three

Depressive Thinking Styles

⬦

This section focuses on the detriment derived from disproportionately and erroneously attributing blame to oneself for the cause of negative occurrences. *Self-deprecation is the condemnation of oneself for unwanted outcomes. It is the common inner dialogue of the depressed mind.* Cognitive theory relating to depression suggests that internalizing responsibility for unwanted circumstances is a key component in the development of a depressive episode. Severity of the depressive condition is related to the degree and exclusivity that one attributes self blame for negative occurrences. This theory and related research indicates that depressed people not only blame themselves disproportionately in relation to the reality of their contribution to the circumstances, but also dwell on it in excess (Beck, et. al., 1979).

Excessive Ruminations

Negative and self-focused thought is particularly potent in instigating intense feelings of depression. The more time spent on dwelling upon self-suffering, attributing blame to self, appraising inadequacy, tallying accounts of past failures, and enumerating personal weaknesses, the more intense and robust the depressive episode. Persons who experience similar unfortunate circumstances, but do not focus persistently on the impact, suffer less incidences of clinical depression. *If one can be successful in diverting attention away from self after disturbing circumstances, the probability of a depressive episode is lessened.*

Depressed people find it very difficult to shift their thinking away from their suffering. They ruminate and try to figure out what they should have done differently. They absorb a lot of blame. They spend enormous amounts of time thinking about their shortcomings and worthlessness. They wallow in the misery of their suffering and, in course, are unlikely to realize brighter points of view that might surface as a consequence of looking at the circumstance from a distance. They see themselves as the center of the universe where disastrous situations have converged. It is this very short sightedness that keeps the depressed person from discovering perspectives that grant access to more positive appraisals of self. This *perpetual immersion of self into pity and sorrowfulness increases the degree of suffering and may prolong the course of depression.*

Conscious distraction away from continual self focus lessens pejorative judgments and allows a therapeutic advantage of introducing complicit external factors that help to mitigate feelings of total responsibility. Although it may be instinctive to lick one's wounds, a strong benefit is achieved by distancing oneself from repeatedly re-experiencing the play-by-play of the life event precipitating depressive feelings. To continue to deliberate on things beyond one's control is an exercise in futility. This is perhaps why so many people have benefited from the Serenity Prayer.

This next poem shuns away maladaptive self indulgence. It reminds us that *self care is not synonymous with self absorption.* It promotes a wellness behavior and mentality.

It suggests the benefits of letting go of anal thinking that seeks to find rational explanations for every condition of life. It breathes a sigh of relief that flows from the acknowledgement that the human condition is frequently without self sufficiency and understanding. It culminates in a spiritual mindedness that relinquishes personal control and turns over the consideration of people, places and things to God.

Prescription: Recite as needed to resist the natural tendency to keep revisiting the source and experience of injury. It is especially efficacious in assisting the depressed one to stop sabotaging the healing process.

Woe Is Me

Woe is me
Depression thrives on self-pity
Continually focusing on the experience of grief
Constantly recalling the disbelief.

Can't listen to the world calling from the outside
Too preoccupied with what's going on inside
The "I" of the storm dominates the news
Flash! Coming up! Details on the inner city blues.

Constant introspection limits the ability of the fox
To be crafty and think outside of the box
Problem solving requires a fresh locus
New inspiration, an external focus.

Positive distraction away from oneself
Affords the opportunity to improve the mind's health
Increased attention to the external view
Offers promise, provides balance, a chance to
        renew.

The severity of the depressed mood
Is relative to the time given to brood
Self absorption with sorrowful thought
Leads to more confusion and feeling distraught.

Blue is the timbre of a sad refrain
A discord struck over and over again
To find comfort in the staff and the rod
The mantra becomes "Let go and let God!"

Chapter Four

Conditions and Events Associated with Depression

⬥

Loneliness

One of the most difficult challenges to endure is the condition of loneliness. Loneliness and depression present the same faces. Frequently, they are overlapping conditions (Booth, 1992). Loneliness may bring about some of the same self-criticalness, negative outlooks, appearances of sadness and emptiness symptomatic of depression. Depression tends to be more global while loneliness is restricted to interpersonal disappointment and hurt unless the two conditions overlap. Often, loneliness is the result of a failed relationship or loss. Although not required, loneliness may be accompanied by feelings of guilt, hopelessness, and traumatic memories identical to symptoms associated with a depressive condition. Loneliness, as a condition, represents a more severe degree of suffering than the "blue achoo" described earlier, but is not as limiting as a full-blown case of depression that includes loneliness. Nevertheless, it proves very difficult to endure because we thrive so much on human contact and discourse.

Loneliness can readily impair psychological functioning. It may distort thinking, temperament, and perceptions of social and interpersonal relations (Booth, 1992). Loneliness, in general, fosters a quality of thinking that perpetuates behaviors that further disassociate lonely persons from social involvement. *Loneliness behaviors often develop into characteristic patterns of behaviors that can make a person more prone to a full-blown case of depression* or helps to sustain a chronic episode of depression. Loneliness as a condition can readily impair the functionality of personality and result in reduced access to friends and other sources of support. Commonly, loneliness is the result of broken relationships that leaves a person feeling dejected, wounded, and afraid to venture into the relationship arena again. Depending upon the degree of severity, this disappointing life event can precipitate a clinical depressive episode if other factors of susceptibility are present. Approximately *30 to 40 percent of divorced persons report an increase of depressive symptoms, and people who encounter relationship tragedies double the risk of developing a depressive disorder* (Brown & Harris, 1989). *It is important for people who suffer from loneliness to challenge themselves to break out of asocial behaviors* that ultimately increase feelings of inadequacy, emptiness, and overlapping symptoms of depression.

The next poem speaks to lonely hearts. It relates to one of the more common stressful life events associated with a depressive episode. The poem reflects feelings of loneliness that results from the loss of an intimate partner. It suggests the process and steps necessary to come out of the state of sadness associated with this kind of loss and start new and promising relationships that may bring about a return to happiness.

Prescription: This poem is to be read twice a day, mornings and evenings, to encourage a greater desire to increase social contact and activity. It rallies a call to action to become more engaged in developing new relationships, eventually leading to filling the void of loss of intimacy. Data show (Grissom, 1996) a 1:4 ratio of time needed for healing in relation to time spent in relationship. That is, for every 4 years in a serious relationship, a year of healing is required to recover from the loss. The poem assumes that a sufficient amount of time has been given to practices promoting healing and recovery from a broken relationship prior to seeking to engage a new romantic relationship.

Loneliness Condition

Yearning for the presence of one
To fill my desire for a companion
Someone to share happiness
A partner during times of spoiled success

Wanting a sense of comfort and a familiar touch
Laughter, conversation would be appreciated very
    much
Not having to pretend and put on airs
Knowing I have someone who truly cares

I miss the stir of your morning rise
The gentleness of your soul peering through your
    eyes
I long for the chemistry of a noontime caress
Caring words softly spoken and filled with
    tenderness

I ache for the small things
That day through night togetherness brings
I miss the intimacies that preceded divorce
The sharing of love during sexual intercourse

Again, I desire to be in a committed relationship
The connectedness of having someone at my hip
My mind is in need of mental stimulation
The kind that comes from human relation

Feeling insecure about my package
Will I be seen as having too much baggage?
I doubt my attractiveness and ability to compete
Can I find someone who is truthful, kind, and sweet?

Afraid I'll never love again
Unnerved by the idea of finding a new friend
Don't want to get out there to look around
Negative thinking puts me down

The thought of initiating contact increases my stress
With every missed opportunity, feeling more
    hopeless
Cannot allow myself to go on like this
All of what I desire is what I will miss

I'll have to take the risk of opening the door
To allow a process to find what I'm looking for
Reduce the expectations of someone I wish to clone
Discover positive aspects of spending time alone

I will reach out to others without their knowing
I'm overcoming loneliness by being outgoing
I will awaken a spirit of interpersonal exchange
I'll respond to cues within my range

I will inch toward the intimacy I seek
I will gain strength from having been weak
I will introduce myself to new possibilities
I will put my lonely heart at ease.

Loss

Loss of a Loved One

Relationship maladies are potent triggers for a depressive episode. The death of a spouse, family member or friend represents an avalanche of dreary precipitation that is likely to drench positive manifestations of mood. Psychological distress resulting from bereavement is powerfully incapacitating (Brown & Moran, 1997). This kind of loss, not uncommonly, fosters prolonged emotional despair. *Approximately 25 percent of those who suffer from depression after the death of a spouse are still suffering 6 months after the death.* Fortunately, the incidence of depression after 18 months dramatically declines (Zisook & Shuchter 1991).

Those who experienced equitable and amicable relationships before their loss tend to fare better. They are more readily able to draw from pleasurable memories as a source of consolation. *Those who are able to accept that losses are a sad but natural course of life, do not dwell on concepts such as unfairness, and are able to find productive endeavors as they attempt to recover tend to have greater resiliency* (Carr, Neese, & Wortman, 2006).

The next poem depicts the experience of loss of a spouse or partner. It is a narrative of the sorrow, grief, and new beginning of living through the first year after the death of someone special. It covers the stages of grieving (Kluber-Ross, 1969). It captures a pivotal piece of the grieving process, the need to remember and share the positive memories of the deceased. *Those supporting the grieving person are reminded to avail themselves to listen, and encourage the expression of his or her highlights of personal history as a means of providing forums for potential catharsis.*

Prescription: This poem is potent. It provides an emotional outlet for the positive expression of mourning and grief. The frequency of reading will vary according to the individual. Use as needed.

Remembering

I used to buy fruit tarts for two
Today I only bought one.
It tastes the same but eating it was not as fun.
I didn't hear the "mmm this is good" you would say
*   when you had your first bite.*
Knowing I had given you a small joy always
*   brought my heart delight.*
Most times there would be an exchange of glances
*   as we slowly spooned in.*
It seemed to help savor the flavor with my lover and
*   friend*
It's hard to stop thinking about the special times we
*   knew*
I wish the Lord had taken me instead of taking you
Empty is my present, so rich is my past
My memories of you will forever last
I need to tell our stories every chance I get
From the beginning of our sunrise to the end of our
*   sunset*

Grieving and Mourning

The grieving process is necessary to accommodate the real life meaning of loss as a devastating occurrence. Mourning is a continuation of the grieving process and helps the saddened heart to gain a new perspective about his or her changed life so that he or she may again reintegrate into a society of the living. During the grieving or mourning processes, some will inevitably experience the intensity and duration of symptoms characteristic of an episode of clinical depression. They should seek professional help and support.

Mourning is an extended process and for some it may last many months or years. It helps the person suffering a loss (death or severance of a relationship) to release the ties that were binding the relationship. *Mourning helps bring into realization the need to adapt to a new world reality. It points the way to living healthily in a reconfigured social context that offers meaning and relation as an uncertain future unfolds* (Rando, 1995). There are several important adjustments and behaviors to be accomplished over the course of mourning to avoid complications, including severe depression.

Healthy mourning requires coming to grips with the loss, its causes, and implications. It entails getting in touch with feelings of anguish and sorrow and committing to a process of working through these emotions. *Mourning is a process of reaching out for memories and experiences that were a vital part of the history of the relationship. At the same time, it suggests the need to let go of the expectations associated with the previous context and to find a way of suiting up for new experiences without having to negate the essence and appeal of what has passed.* Finally, mourning calls for looking ahead at a path of future purpose and meaning that is always present for the living. However, this may prove especially challenging for those who have built their lives around someone and are subsequently at a loss as to how to move forward without them. They will benefit most from a support system that recognizes the need for assistance over an extended period in finding a way back into a mainstream of life that allows them to establish new ties while still respecting the importance of maintaining rituals and remembrances of gone, but not forgotten relationships (Rando, 1995).

The following poem depicts the kind of inner dialogue that one may healthily engage in while working through stages of grief and mourning periods. It validates mental states of confusion and feelings of despair. It solicits memories that help to ensure the reality of the loss is not denied. The poem encourages concerted effort to find meaning, purpose, belonging, and a recommitment to living life with zeal.

Prescription: This poem is for that period of time when intense grieving has lessened; however, the sorrow and agony of loss still persist. It is for comfort and meditation when the level of company and support has dwindled and the reality of disconnectedness sets in. Read this poem in the morning to embrace the reality and promise of a new life.

Life After Loss (Healthy Mourning)

The small things loom large when I'm alone
Memories of trivia we've known
Reflections of time well spent
Makes my loss less of a lament
The reality of death cannot be undone
The treasures of the past sustains this one

Unimaginable to think
So much can happen in a blink
Reminded of you at every turn
Each night a candle I burn
Struggling to realize the bond is broken
Unfulfilled dreams go unspoken

Call it grieving but it's suffering from disbelieving
Wish to embrace the vivid memories I'm retrieving
Very difficult adjusting to a world minus you
My planned future will never come true
Anguishing over the incredible hurt
Of watching your coffin sink into the dirt

Now I must resolve to live
To offer to others what I have to give
Find social comfort, gain some peace
Channel my feelings through a positive release
As I put my life back into a forward gear
I accept that a major part of me died this year

Suicidal Ideations and Behaviors

Depression is a very disparaging disorder. It communicates that one no longer has adequate resources to manage the intense despair resulting from an awful life event. It is a time when one realizes a frailty of mind, body, and spirit. It's a time of reckoning. It is a very humbling emotional state where it should become abundantly clear that the ship is going to sink without external sources of help. It is here that the suffering person would be wise to admit to a lack of personal resources and seek help. However, many put off asking for help until the situation has advanced to a critical stage. It's akin to not properly treating the flu until it compromises the immune system and instigates the development of infection to allow for the advance of life threatening conditions, such as pneumonia.

When suffering reaches a point of dejection and correspondingly dampens the desire to live, it has progressed to a place of emergency and is in need of a therapeutic response. It is a time to surrender one's own mechanisms of dealing with the crises to levels of interventions of greater expertise. For some, asking for help from an outside source is enormously challenging. They cannot relinquish self management of the circumstances. Many believe that admitting to a lack of ability to handle one's own problems is the epitome of weakness and represents a state of sickness worse than the causes of suffering in the first place.

Many who assume this stance of belief attempt to control their pain by taking drugs and alcohol to numb the effect. For the most part, this only worsens their predicament as it allows the problems to fester during a time when possible solutions are delayed by this denial and distraction. The need that some depressed people have to stay in sole control of their circumstances may be dangerously self defeating. It sometimes leads to very tragic outcomes. At the core of depression is the realization that there are overwhelming conditions that are not remitting despite the best efforts of the suffering person. In the sufferer's mind, he or she is using every method they have or can make available to resolve the issues plaguing them.

Sadly, the depressed person relying solely upon his or her own resources may come to a point where there is no vision of improvement or resolution of the severe emotional suffering. At this point, he or she may yield to a state of hopelessness that permits a decision to end the episode of suffering by committing suicide (Freeman, and Reinecke, 1993). To those of us wanting to help and care for persons suffering so intensely, this is one of the most frightening possibilities of depressed thinking and behavior. It is hoped that depressed persons who are at their wits end to solve their misery can find connection to a source of relief and healing that offers an appeal that he or she finds reasonable and prevents an act of absolute finality.

This next poem speaks to the pain, suffering, and hopelessness that instigate suicidal ideations. It identifies with the desperation common to persons who contemplate, attempt, and commit suicide. It encourages the sufferer to seek therapeutic help to live rather than opting to seek death as a solution to the intense despair.

Prescription: Read, as needed, to counter suicidal thinking. Pay special attention to the hopefulness that is offered by the passage of time and the help afforded by caring persons, especially those practicing in the healing arts professions.

Suicide

The rarely spoken threat
The most unthinkable mindset
A subject difficult to broach
After many paths, the final approach

Horrible suffering
Unsuccessful buffering
Hopeless future
Can't endure

The intensity of pain
Greater than the heart can sustain
Today offers no solution
Ominous thoughts of self-execution

Lack of resource
No conceivable recourse
First a thought, then a plan
Gather the means at hand

Enduring hopelessness
No observable progress
Illness, loss, relational discord
Loneliness, confusion, things one can't afford

Time holds the key to problems solved
There is a future date by which things will be resolved.
Time stands between today's worst and tomorrow's
*   best*
Tolerating the immediate defeat is the essential test

Make a promise that commits to waiting
Tell someone about what you've been contemplating
Share your frustration with living and your
    penchant for dying
Surrender to the truth you've been denying

Reach out for help; expose your pain
Give words to the things that drive you insane
There's a hotline awaiting your call
A counselor, pastor, or friend ready to hear it all

Despair Contamination

Death caused by suicide will undoubtedly have a very strong impact on significant others, family, friends, and coworkers, as well as those professionals with whom therapeutic relationships had been established. Any of these *survivors may subsequently become depressed. Intense feelings of guilt, inadequacy, shame, anger, loss, punishment, and stigma are common to survivors of persons who have committed suicide.* It is very important that these survivors not withdraw from others who are good sources of support. It is best that survivors seek psychotherapeutic and spiritual help to assist them with overcoming the pain and turmoil associated with such a passing (Freeman and Reinecke, 1993).

There is often a sense of rage and terror associated with death by suicide. Generally, there is a continual replay of how it occurred, in all of its gory details. The perceived senselessness and selfishness of the act may indeed complicate the grieving process. Not uncommon, one's grief may frequently be supplanted by anger that such an act could be thought of and carried out without regard to the impact it would have on its survivors. Survivors need a forum for emotional expression and venting of feelings to empathic persons offering understanding and non-judgment.

Survivors must be careful not to shut themselves off from their outside and inside worlds, and allow the course of mourning appropriate channels to find a flow back to homeostasis. During the period of mourning, there is a need for survivors to find meaning in the life and loss of the deceased. In many instances, they need to release themselves from the guilt and responsibility of the actions of the suicide victim. They also need to be able to express feelings of loss and remembrance that are tainted by the intentionality of the death. *It is necessary for survivors to accept their limited ability to control the behavior of others and their greater ability to take control of their own lives.* Often, they require help to appreciate their good qualities and prospects for the future despite the traumatic occurrence. It is important that survivors learn from the experience of the deceased and avail him or herself to the community of support available to those who seek help. Without concentrated, therapeutic care, survivors of suicide are prone to develop and have trouble remitting depressive symptoms.

The next poem identifies with the horrors both in images and feelings that torment the minds of survivors of suicide. It beckons the survivor to work toward resiliency by developing perspectives that foster a greater appreciation of life, releases one from connections to responsibility for the act, and encourages motivation to engage the services of the healing arts community.

Prescription: Read this poem in the morning upon rising and before retiring at night during the grieving and mourning periods following the suicide of someone close.

You're Gone... We're Here

Where your pain has ended, mine has just begun
Can't believe you took your own life with the
squeeze of a gun
The misery you knew will never burden you again
But for me the song of your torment will be a
constant refrain

Saw you drifting, going slowly down the hill
Never imagined you would surrender to a bottle of
pills
You've escaped the jagged edge of this life's agony
But for us the portrait of your dark clouds will
never set us free

Didn't take it seriously, the threatening chorus that
was sung
Went to find you the next morning and there you
hung
Horror froze my body, words I could not speak
You must not have known all the havoc you would
wreak

Your life was our road map before it took a terrible
twist
Hard to understand the thoughts that made you cut
your wrists
Your letter said we'd be better off without you
But your legacy of abandonment leaves your kids
confused

And yet

We must work through feelings of guilt,
As we sew together the cloths of your memory quilt
We must learn to forgive you
For what you chose to do

We must seek help to address our sense of blame
Can't turn away from our support because of our
shame
We must release the beast of anger inside
Not seek to isolate because of wounded pride

We must overcome feelings of inadequacy and
helplessness
We need empathic ears to get things off our chest
We must seek meaning as a part of our daily prayer
You're gone, we're here, and we need care

Chapter Five

Coping with Depression

⤬

If It Doesn't Kill You
It'll Make You Grow!

Long-term memory does not like to store traumatic events that are enormously disturbing, raw, uncensored, and pose an ongoing threat. These events require editing, revision, and new contexts to make them more agreeable with one's understanding of how life is supposed to unfold (Baumeister and Vohs, 2005). Often, traumatic circumstances and events that are at the core of depressive episodes remain in the ruminative stage because they persist in causing a great deal of suffering, anguish, and fear as presently conceptualized. Once repackaged in a more palatable form, they can be stored in long-term memory. This is most readily accomplished by examining the unwanted conditions to derive a means of acquiring meaning, positive transformation, or purposeful results from its occurrence. This is what is encouraged in James 1: 2-3 of the New Testament of the Bible: *Count it all joy when ye fall into diverse temptations (unwanted conditions and trials); knowing this, that the trying of your faith worketh patience.*

71

When distressing life events are conceptualized as imposed or coincidental opportunities for personal development, the corresponding mental and physical health maladies are experienced with less severity and often with more positive outcomes (Baumeister and Vohs, 2005). This suggests it is helpful to find a deliberate process to objectify distress and learn from it. Some find it helpful to write about depressing circumstances. Those who are therapeutically supported through this process have greater resiliency. Therapeutic journaling provides a tool to document growth and eventually conceptualize the disparaging experiences as training and preparing for future challenges in life.

Emotional tragedy and disappointment are extremely painful and difficult to overcome when it appears to be vicious and destructive. However, *when a person can find meaning and purpose that suggests an eventual betterment of self, he or she can begin to shift the focus away from the current suffering to a future state where one can see oneself as having evolved favorably*. From this perspective, disparaging conditions only represent passages that are a part of a bigger process in which people grow wiser and more developed. This promotes optimism during low points in life where the high points are more fully realized and appreciated as a result of the value added during the journey to get there. Thus, finding meaning in displeasing or unwanted occurrences provides a source of improved acceptance and relief from the resulting pain and suffering.

Looking at an undesirable life event as a fleeting segment of time occurring on a continuum of life events that prepare us for future celebrations is a "reframed" perspective. It affords a robust boost to the emotional immune system. Closely related to this concept is the theory of constructivism, which says that *we help to shape our destiny according to how we respond to important life events* (Mahoney, 2005). Evolution itself is predicated upon our making adaptive responses to things that threaten our existence. If we are able to survive destructive assaults, the continuum of life's occurrences will inevitably offer new windows of opportunity as we proceed down its course. This understanding encourages hopefulness, and allows for a commitment to forge ahead with an expectancy that the spoils of sustained effort and vigor will manifest appreciably in the not-too-distant future.

The following poem reprograms pessimistic thoughts. It encourages forward thinking with positive expectation. The poem needs to be hardwired into the core belief system. Consequently, it is necessary to commit it to memory. It espouses an optimistic philosophy about life. The poem should be spoken in verses or entirely as a part of self talk or exchange with others when negative circumstances overwhelm personal resource and diminish the ability to sustain ongoing effort.

Prescription: Read daily during morning meditations. Reaffirm the hopefulness philosophy it represents. This is a medicine for the mind, body, and spirit.

The Continuum

Life is a continuum of events
Surprises, tragedies, rewards, and recompense
A sequence of seasons
Cycling with and without reasons.

Few things are for certain, only His love is for sure
Time resolves all problems, if we can only endure.
Reframe the discomforts and dread of today
Accepting of not having things go your way.

A truism that portends for all
Bumps along the road, a slip and fall
Look forward and anticipate the tomorrow
That reverses the tide of today's sorrow.

Days bring us closer to where something ends
And at that ending moment a new thing begins.
This is most encouraging during times of strife
An anticipation of relief, a renewal of life.

The journal has many entries
Chronicles of blahs, joys and miseries
Remain hopeful! There are many volumes to sum
Promise lies ahead as we journey life's continuum.

Going the Distance

Although there is a considerable measure of optimism generated by the realization that depression is time based, for many it is still extremely difficult to make it through the period of time necessary for depression to run its course. It is the day-to-day drudgery of living with unwanted conditions that makes the prospects of better days ahead seem like a farfetched reality. A lack of mental clarity often prevents the depressed person from accessing a logic that would realize the temporal aspects of the depressing circumstances. In addition, understanding the transience of the process is not sufficient. There are tools and strategies required to get through a depressive episode, not unlike those needed to run a successful marathon. The question that begs is how does one direct his or her paths and bear the anguish and pain during the span of temporariness of depression?

Surviving the Course

Often the depressed person cannot think very far ahead. Therefore, the concept of temporariness of suffering has little meaning unless it applies to the next hour or sometime later in the day. Frequently, clients will tell me "I could hardly wait to get to my therapy session," indicating the difficulty of enduring a moderately short period of time. By definition, clinical depression is established by a prolonged occurrence of symptoms that are characterized by severe sadness, emptiness, anguish, and difficulty coping with several highly accentuated, negative aspects of life. When the depressed person has trouble getting past a weekend, holiday, or any small block of time, she needs strategies and perspectives that allow her to cope with and navigate through the timeframe that encapsulates the course of suffering.

To deny that a course of depression is extremely challenging to endure would be disingenuous. After taking a few strides forward, there will also be many days where the process of coping may seem too formidable. It may feel like the bubble has burst and the foundation has once again collapsed. The sufferer must have an assurance that the course of the depression can be journeyed by using prescribed tools to survive its rigor.

The key element to overcoming a depressive episode is endurance. However, endurance does not come easily. It takes effort, strategy, patience, and a presence of mind. Enduring must be considered a proactive process, where one resists his or her natural inclinations. There is a strong tendency to give in to the weight of depression because it depletes cognitive and physical energy as it applies its gravity. If one surrenders and does not employ strategies and techniques that promote endurance; dreadful outcomes may ensue, which I will talk about later in the book. On the other hand, if one can little-by-little, day-by-day incrementally advance the struggle, then a profitable outcome will be achieved. It is through this daily process of exercising proactive thinking and behavior that stamina is developed. At first, like the first few weeks of exercising, there may not be any perceptible change. However, as time progresses and effort is consistently made, the ability to endure becomes more pronounced.

The next poem encourages endurance over the course of a depressive episode. It is very powerful. It gives instruction and encouragement to manage days when the inclination to give up is strong. God inspired me to write this poem to provide inspiration to those who are desperate in their endeavors to maintain steadfastness to the process of overcoming depression. The poem provides a stabilizing set of principles and ethics that helps one to recommit to the struggle of prevailing against difficult to bear circumstances. It encourages and instructs anyone going through drama and psychological distress to rely upon its helpful strategies to sustain endurance while in the depths of a difficult phase. It is a poem that I've gone to many times to assist me in coping with personal challenges.

Prescription: This poem is to be read two or more times a day during the phase of depression where the incentive to move forward is low. It is worthwhile to memorize this poem as it will prove to be a source of inspiration that encourages on those days when personal resolve is empty. It is an anthem that rallies the mind and spirit to keep advancing purposefully through minutes, hours, days, and longer periods to arrive at a place of greater promise.

The One Who Endures

Going the distance is the difficult part
The adrenalin makes it not so apparent at the very
*   start*
When the pain and misery continue to persist
The will to move on begins to diminish

A strategic course of action assures a discipline
To guide one through the winding road that never
*   seems to end*
A steady pace of strides with determination
Gradually reduces the remoteness of the destination

The one who endures tolerates discomfort and pain
Is not discouraged by the lack of apparent gain
Accepts the time it takes
Until time decides to apply the brakes

Looks to the near and not to the far
Focuses on the positives in the way things are
Is distracted away from the place of injury
Pursues constructive preoccupation and activity

Finds a source of comfort and peace
An outlet for tension and frustration release
Keeps feelings of failure in tow
Realizes the opportunity to grow

Increases personal strength through perseverance
Adapts to the commotion of each circumstance
Responds to the need to nourish the self
Maintains a reserve to handle the unexpected
*   stealth*

Avoids the grimace when not having fun
Commits to the many phases of the long run
Delays immediate gratification for a bigger benefit
Resists the urge to give up and quit

Chapter Six

Treatment of Depression

Cognitive-Behavioral Therapy

Cognitive-behavioral therapy (CBT) has been shown to be a very effective psychotherapy for the treatment of depression. This type of psychotherapy emphasizes the challenging of beliefs and practices that promote, amplify, or sustain depression. Each of us has core beliefs and philosophies about life, people, and events that strongly influence how we make sense of our experiences. The occurrence of unfortunate events often shapes our beliefs and frames of references in maladaptive ways, producing distorted thoughts and perceptions. These irrational and misguided cognitions become defaults that we resort to when related events and situations occur. Instigating circumstances automatically trigger the defaults into executive action to explain what is happening and how one should respond. Defaults that are based on erroneous assumptions and ill-conceived interpretations lead to negative assessments and maladaptive behavior. For example, the following is a distorted core belief: "There is something about me that makes dishonest people seek me out." As a consequence of this belief, whenever this person encounters a dishonest person (as inevitably

81

we all must), she blames herself for being the person that attracts this element, rather than assigning sole responsibility to the dishonest person. A person prone to depression will routinely attribute the cause of unwanted conditions to him or herself. He or she frequently generalizes negative circumstance(s) to global proportions, and anticipates that the future will yield ongoing dissatisfaction.

The Power of Two Minds

If there was ever a time when two heads were better than one, it would be when the depressed person becomes immersed in the repetitive analysis of negative information. It is here that his mind becomes bogged down with tunnel-vision focused on negative perspectives that fuel firestorms of misery and devastation. Alone, the depressed person loses capacity to defend against harsh indictments, many of which may be self inflicted. It is not that the depressed mind is incapable of productive rebuttal, but rather the content of thought is filtered by a narrowly focused range of explanation. Hence, points of view considered are often impoverished.

It has been well established that a cogent mind is needed to battle depression. However, maintaining an objective and resourceful mind during sorrowful circumstances is challenging. Often, it is extremely difficult to focus the lens of the mind to a setting appropriate to bring about therapeutic change. *The depressed mind sees negative information with the clarity of a magnification instrument.* It is like looking at your face with a magnification mirror. The blemishes and pimples are more unsightly than in the normal reflection. Similarly, *the depressed person generally finds it difficult to appreciate many of the positive possibilities that are available because of the exaggerated ugliness of life's challenging circumstances.* As a result, the depressed person will likely need the help of someone outside of herself to call attention to competitive appraisals that offer greater promise and hope.

If the depressed person can be coaxed to entertain and internalize brighter, more hopeful perspectives, then the degree of severity of gloom can be appreciably decreased. Frustration and hopelessness resulting from lack of resolve can be overturned. This requires a collaborative process where the depressed person joins with another to consider alternative possibilities. This process of combined effort to brainstorm solutions to extremely difficult life challenges is vital to changing illness mentality to wellness mentality. Therapists trained in cognitive-behavioral therapy and other modalities that treat depression are best trained to join in collaboration with those suffering to find brighter, more optimistic perspectives that help to lift the veil of depression.

The next poem underscores the importance of working with others to arrive at perspectives that realize a potential for circumstance reframing or improvement. *Reframing involves redefining a circumstance in such a way that it takes on another implication that gives rise to more promising possibilities and increased hopefulness.*

Prescription: Recite one time a day prior to connecting to a therapist or counselor.

83

Don't Brainstorm Alone

Two heads are better than one
Problem solving is best accomplished by
*   collaboration*
Therapy is a meeting of the minds
To relieve hurt, guilt, pain, and shame that binds

Confusion is at the heart of every crisis
A failure to find conflict resolution devices
Solo ruminations yield diminishing returns
United thinking resolves complicated concerns

Accepting another into one's private domain
Requires a respect and sense of trust to attain
Healing strategies multiply when there're two to
*   hone*
Therapy works! Don't brainstorm alone.

Uplift the Mind and the Mood will follow

CBT illustrates how faulty thinking and conclusions help to precipitate corresponding negative feelings and moods. CBT challenges the basic notions that support depressed feelings by requiring the affected person to substantiate his or her rationales in light of other perspectives that are demonstrated to have a greater basis in reality. *CBT appeals to the depressed person to discontinue a system of belief if the evidence does not prove it to be valid.* Ultimately, it provides the depressed person with the power to improve her low state of being by exercising the mind's positive capacity to effect emotions.

The following poem illustrates the efficacious impact the mind can have on the experience of depression. This is expressly developed in the Mind Over Mood Workbook (Greenberger and Padesky, 1995).

Prescription: This poem is to be recited daily as a preamble to cognitive therapy homework or workbook exercises.

The Mind Can Overrule the Mood

The mind generates many scenarios
To explain one circumstance
The objective is to select only those
Supported by arguments of substance

Thoughts are automatic
Responses to things we feel
Distorted thoughts follow a logic
Based on assumptions not real

The depressed mind exaggerates the negative
Hard pressed to grasp the brighter point of view
Puts a strain on the thrust to live
Sees a major catastrophe from a small snafu

Overcoming depressive thinking via a practical
*   exercise:*
Does the stream of thought make sense?
Is there astigmatism of the eyes?
Is the hypothesis supported by evidence?

Depression is a response to a dark, dreadful plot
Only sorrowful words can depict
The mind does best to suggest what's not
Writing a more uplifting script

The mind should be a compass
To direct the proper course
Steering away from misguided paths
As it considers every source

Filtering out the rays of gloom
Promising prospects can be viewed
Eliminating false evidence to assume
The mind can overrule the mood

CBT Interventions

The following procedures and modifications of thinking constitute the essential components of cognitive-behavioral therapy. The interventions are divided into cognitive and behavioral approaches.

Cognitive Interventions:

1. Challenging Maladaptive Thinking

As the depressed individual becomes more active, she gains greater capacity to question the beliefs supporting her depressive styles of thinking. However, this requires conscious effort and is usually facilitated through therapy. Dreadful, negatively oriented, pessimistic styles of thinking sustain depressed feelings and moods. Generally, there is dissatisfaction with self, circumstances, and outlook for the future (Beck, et. al., 1979). *The depressed person must learn to query and authenticate his or her core beliefs and not just automatically respond to negative persuasions.* If not, these core beliefs are likely to generate self-fulfilling prophesies.

Everyone experiences emotional injuries and scarring. *Psychological suffering is directly proportionate to the degree of vulnerability present when trauma occurs. Vulnerability is fostered by preconceived, negative notions that one does not possess sufficient competency or adequacy to be successful in certain challenging circumstances.* The vulnerability generally voices expectations of failure. When distressful circumstances and activation of vulnerability crisscross each other, the potential for a depressive episode is created. If the disparaging conditions precipitate self-deprecating thoughts (put downs, feelings of inadequacy, low self esteem), pervasive dissatisfaction with current circumstances, and global pessimism, the person is likely to succumb to the vulnerability, thus increasing the intensity of the insult and possibility of a severe depressive episode.

When events occur that challenge well being and match the content found in an area of vulnerability, the suscepti- bility to injury is increased. For example, a self-made busi- ness person has the notion that a formally educated person is afforded greater opportunities than the street-smart person. He may be constantly expecting unfavorable decisions and outcomes based on longstanding beliefs. His negative bias may cause him to minimize the consideration of his positive qualities and experience.

When his business is challenged, and a formally educated competitor outdistances him, he may take it very person- ally. A downward spiral may follow, causing a plummet into further pessimism and self doubt that eventually leads to a depressive episode. If, however, the validity of his conclu- sions can be refuted by showcasing the successes of others with backgrounds similar to his, then his unsubstantiated automatic thoughts may give way to thinking that promotes a drive toward resiliency and recommitment after an unsuc- cessful venture. ***When the evidence does support the conclu- sion, the verdict must be overturned.***

The next poem illustrates how the mind can fall prey to thinking that erroneously and unnecessarily leads to exag- gerated, gloom-and-doom conclusions.

Prescription: Read this poem daily during the early phase of realizing feelings of depression. It affords insight and inspiration toward recovery.

Musing of the Mind

Negative notions are
Building blocks
Steps to realizing
Expected realities
As life serves a variety of plates
Likely not to like some
When the spoiled dish tops the menu
Confirms cynical beliefs tightly held
Can't see the forest of hopefulness
For the trees of despair
The storm of thoughts
Become a hurricane
Skies darken
Strong winds blow
Torrential rains douse
Handicapping strategies
Foil adaptive strides
Weak foundations uprooted

The moral?
Style of thinking
Shapes the unfolding of events
However,
The course may be re-routed
According to
The musing of the mind

2. Adjusting Distorted Thinking

As stated earlier, many depressed people feel they are being conscientious in assuming blame for things gone wrong. There is a natural inclination to want to discover the causes of disappointments; however, *in attempting to explore the role that one played in causing an unwanted circumstance to occur, there is often too much focus on implicating oneself as the sole agent of responsibility.* This method of thinking is frequently reinforced by others in an effort to get the depressed person to claim ownership of his or her surreptitious participation. This proves unfortunate when what is heard is the reiteration of a negative appraisal of the depressed individual that justifies the occurrence of the unwanted event. *The depressive experience is deepened if the attribution of blame is realized as belonging solely to the person suffering.*

It is self damaging for injured persons to continually ruminate about his or her perceived instigation of a malady. What is actually called for is objectivity and reality checking. Acceptance of a role in most of our life events is healthy. However, when one assails dire situations as a reflection of his behavior and mentality, he or she loses an accurate perception of reality. A distortion of thinking can readily suggest that all negative outcomes are attributable to the sufferer. This defies logic and fosters an overwhelming sense of sorrow, dejection, hopelessness, and unworthiness (Beck, et. al., 1979). *No one person gives rise to all of the conditions and causes of disconcerting life events. Persons who are able to attribute some of the causality of negative outcomes to external sources (as well as, see these negative conditions as temporary) tend to be less encumbered in attaining important goals and accomplishments that bring personal satisfaction, and refute depressive thinking* (Gibb, Zhu, Alloy, & Abramson, 2002). There is a benefit from actively searching for people and things that share the responsibility for unfavorable life circumstances.

The following poem encourages the conflicted person to share responsibility for unwanted circumstances. It suggests thinking that dares to implicate ill fate and other people as culprits in concocting a recipe for emotional suffering. It gives permission to point the finger away from self and consequently avoid a tendency, characteristic of the depressed mind, to exclaim "It's entirely my fault." It intimates a benefit from actively searching for people and things that share the responsibility for unfavorable life circumstances. It reduces feelings of guilt and shame.

Prescription: Recite this poem throughout the day immediately after an occurrence that precipitates depression, and then as needed. It is especially useful during those moments when the mind insists on generating indictments that allege you are solely responsible for the circumstances that cause your suffering.

It's Not all On You!

Down in the dumps
Down on self
Anguish from life's lumps
Hit below the belt

Carrying the brunt of the burden
Owning the causes of the mood
Belaboring mistakes with 20-20 vision
Signing off on all problems accrued

But should this be the equation?
The injured takes all the blame?
Time to come to the realization
You're just a player and not the game

There's something masochistic about a belief
That suggests it's all on you
Amplifies the experience of misery and grief
Makes self-flagellation the only point of view

Later for that virtue you must dutifully suffer
Says accept responsibility for the web woven
Encourages you to be an anger stuffer
Come on, the sadness was imposed...not chosen

There are multiple causes for the unhappiness
Some outside of your control
Point to people and things away from your vest
They also share liability for what has taken its toll

Don't be the one who shoulders the entire load
That's assuming responsibility to a fault
See other factors contributing to the episode
Too much pepper, but also too much salt

Externalizing Causality

Cognitive-behavioral therapy research shows that depressed people tend to attribute causal responsibility for positive occurrences to external sources while attributing causal responsibility for negative occurrences to themselves. Treatment of depression attempts to invert this relationship to relieve the weight of enormous self deprecation. I sometimes exaggerate the allowance of distancing oneself from causal responsibility for things gone awry to bring about an added comic relief.

It appears very unnatural for a person to turn against oneself. It would seem instinctive for one to maintain thought and behavior that is self preserving. However, this does not always occur. Not unlike an autoimmune disease where the body mistakenly attacks and destroys healthy cells that are needed to maintain the body's well being, depression inclines many to initiate and perpetuate cognitions and behavior inconsistent with emotional health. Hence, the depressed mind frequently produces self-focused attributions that attack self confidence, worth, ability, and optimism and weakens emotional health to the point that it is extremely difficult to thrive. This is an absolute fluke of nature. It is not supposed to happen this way. Everyone should work hard to maintain a level of self protection that allows for the least aversive consequences. It is essential in fighting off and attempting to overcome depression that one uses every cognitive, emotional, and behavioral resource available to not drown in deep waters created by one's own tears. *The burden of depression is lessened as the share or responsibility for its cause is lessened.*

Darwinian Theory suggests we are programmed to attempt to preserve ourselves. We are prone to present ourselves in the most favorable light. Under normal circumstances, we automatically attempt to save ourselves from danger, distress, and disgrace. Many of us will readily misrepresent the facts to avoid negative consequences. I do not advocate lying to achieve a gain or avoid a negative consequence. However, I do suggest that *one gains a therapeutic benefit from acknowledging how other persons or things significantly contribute to undesirable life events during a depressive episode.*

Looking at external sources of complicity is not bad because it is self-serving; it is actually good because it is self-serving. During depressive episodes, one needs as much self-serving strategy as possible. It serves the purpose of diverting attention away from self absorption that focuses primarily on negative self appraisal.

The next poem allows for some comic relief. It suggests it is okay to unload some of the blame onto an external source to accrue a therapeutic benefit. It may not reflect the best character qualities, although it serves to defray inundation with an overwhelming sense of personal responsibility.

Prescription: Recite this poem as needed to instigate primitive instincts that are self protective. It is a lighthearted approach to distancing oneself from self-deprecation.

The Dog Ate My Homework

To avoid harm is instinctive
The mind is constantly reminded
The body wants to live

Good defenses soften the blow
Implicate outside factors
Frames others' pictures to show

As children we automatically knew
Better off to say
Jimmy did it too!

In the beginning, he denied ability to intuit
Adam introduced the first disclaimer
That woman made me do it!

3. Cognitive Restructuring

Thinking that helps to shift focus away from self indictment proves to be very therapeutic in overcoming depression. Attribution theory teaches us that moods can be altered by changing the perspectives of negatively biased thoughts. The essential concept of cognitive therapy is that *thought precedes mood.* The challenge is to get the depressed individual to recognize the need to *change the quality or content of thinking to facilitate healthier perspectives of the circumstances causing negative moods* (Stuart, Blecke, & Renfrow, 2006). Most often, the depressed person is unaware of the direct relationship between quality of thought and mood. Indeed, they see their postulations as real and verifiable. Upon objective examination of these thoughts and thinking patterns, many are found to be distorted and lack support or evidence of validity in reality. The distorted thoughts constitute beliefs that negatively and pejoratively evaluate the self, his or her immediate circumstances, as well as cast doubts about the viability of the self in the future. They result in feelings of intense self loathing, helplessness, and hopelessness.

As thoughts are surfaced, they are given neutral, negative, or positive valences according to how they are emotionally registered. It requires constant work to maintain optimistic thinking when pervasive negativity clouds a positive perspective. However, the work helps to attenuate the severity of a depressed mood. Awareness of the dire consequences of allowing unchecked negative thought content to roam freely around the mind promotes realization of the need to police thought production. As stated earlier, mood is a derivative of thought and can consequently be channeled in euthymic or dysphoric directions according to the valence of the thoughts. Therefore, *one should take caution to monitor thoughts entertained either actively or passively.* This includes thoughts fueled by music, media, and conversation. *CBT's therapeutic strategy is to police negative thinking and "reframe" it with a more positive perspective without essentially changing the factual information.* A classic example would be to view the glass as half full instead of half empty.

The following poem highlights the connections between thoughts and mood. It underscores the implications of allowing negative thoughts to percolate. It advocates deliberate actions to confront and disarm potentially depressing thought content.

Prescription: Read and reread daily until the concepts here are internalized and practiced routinely.

Moods are Subject to Thoughts

Life at times will seem unfair
No matter how well we prepare
There is a choice though of how we conclude
That keeps it together or lets it come unglued

Negative thoughts regarding the self
Are toxins that target emotional health
Generate a downward spiral effect
A beeline for the mood to plummet

Low self regard heightens distress
A potent recipe to hinder success
Thinking that diminishes inner value
Assures depressive feelings to ensue

Control of thought content is essential
Thoughts to feelings is sequential
Try appraising to extract the benefit
Placing emphasis on strength over deficit

Work to inoculate a disturbing belief
Argue against thoughts that support grief
Look to the passing of a wintry season
Persist to find a hopeful voice of reason

4. Challenging Distorted Thinking:

Overcoming Childhood Programming

Often, tendencies to evaluate circumstances toward the negative and realize them as severely detrimental stem back to childhood. *Negative events that produce remarkably negative outcomes over the course of childhood frequently predispose the child toward developing a filtering system that blocks out the positive possibilities and intensifies negative implications.* Negative self images, poor self esteem, feelings of powerlessness, mistrust, and other self limiting, incapacitating core beliefs are by-products of distressing life events created during childhood. Dysfunctional parental, family, peer, community, and cultural practices frequently envelop children and instigate an acceptance of cognitions and predispositions that inappropriately denigrate impressions of self, circumstances, or expectations of the future.

Once ingrained, *childhood beliefs are difficult to change. They develop into cognitive defaults that are reflexively retrieved from the neural network of programming throughout the life span.* Depressogenic thinking is a mindset programming that readily channels streams of thought toward negative appraisals even when circumstances represent neutral or positive considerations (Gibb, et. al., 2002). *Depressogenic thinking disallows a person to see other interpretations that might present a more favorable estimation. Unless the person learns to interrupt the circuitry leading to these corrupted files, he or she will continue to instinctively respond to the negative circumstances in a manner that incubates sorrowful expectations. Additionally, these depressive ideas are called negative schema or negative automatic thoughts in psychological literature* (Beck, et. al., 1979). *Many common folk simply refer to them as "issues."*

The following poem is written in a "blues" song genre. Like the blues, it is an expression of an unpleasant truth that leads to a cathartic relief. Its language is down home and is meant to illicit a bit of laughter. Its humor is designed to have a secondary therapeutic effect. Of course, humor has been found to improve the recovery process in depression and other physical illnesses (Leftcourt, 2005; Cousins, 1979).

Prescription: A nice poem to memorize. It is to be recited prior to engaging in psychotherapy or any self-exploratory, self help work. It will be of benefit when encountering a circumstance that surfaces insecurities or unpleasantness from the past.

Issues: Down Home Blues

Where do they come from?
Faulty programming from when we was young
Life messed up in teaching us lessons
Guaranteed us hard knocks and therapy sessions

Family dysfunction and child abuse
Made stuff normal that breaks the rules
Harsh criticism to build up some character
Didn't consider feelings an important factor

Compared to others, threatened with removal
Bent over backwards to get approval
Love sometimes and sometimes not
Not sure how we earned what we got

Disappointed over and over again
Trust doubtful and suspicion the upper hand
No stability bout what's up week to week
Abandonment, perfectionism, control freak

Self protection determines actions we choose
Some folks call them quirks and label them issues
Down in the dumps we frequently slide
Got so much crap going on inside

'Bout time to bring a change of mind
Leave all those down home hang-ups behind
Figure different the things we confuse
Unlearn the habits that tell our issues

5. Thought Stopping

The ability to monitor and control thinking is of fundamental importance in preventing and overcoming depression. This requires an active mind that automatically works to redress self-sabotaging and pessimistic thinking.

However, when depressed, the mind is less capable of opening up to positive information and tends to dwell on and amplify negative information. It is in this regard that the depressed mind begins to attack itself similar to the case of an autoimmune disease. In severe cases, the mind can become overwhelmed, exhausted, and vulnerable to shutdown and surrender. Here, the mind arrives at a stage of hopelessness. This is a most disturbing condition because it is essential that the mind maintain a survival mode to challenge and rewrite those scripts that set the stage to allow people and events to sap vitality out of life.

All of the strategies and coping mechanisms mentioned throughout this book are dependent upon the mind working actively and productively to save the organism from the throws of harm. Generally, when one arrives at a stage of hopelessness, professional help is required. *The depressed person must be administered encouragement to keep the mind from going dark.* It is readily possible to encourage oneself with mantras and affirmations. Every effort must be put forth to keep the mind committed to the survival of an intact self.

The next poem encourages cerebral fortitude in staving off assaults against mental stamina. How often is one tempted to give up when opposition is persistent? This work provides a powerful refrain to strengthen resolve to maintain sanity during times of extreme challenge.

Prescription: Read this poem through once to identify the particular challenge at hand. Then, recite the line that pertains, along with the refrain, each time the challenge presents itself.

Don't Surrender the Mind

Break in the heart
Don't surrender the mind
Financial woes
Don't surrender the mind
Ton of problems
Don't surrender the mind
Frustration with the occupation
Don't surrender the mind
Decline in health
Don't surrender the mind
Complications with social relations
Don't surrender the mind
Upsetting circumstances
Don't surrender the mind
Mood is subdued
Don't surrender the mind
Overwhelmed by fear and insecurity
Don't surrender the mind
Dreams filled with screams
Don't surrender the mind
Lonely and alone
Don't surrender the mind
The mind is the fountain of hope
Don't surrender the mind

6. Reality Testing

Sometimes there is no way to reframe an ugly picture. "It is what it is" and one has to accept that. Initially, there may be instinctive and even therapeutic efforts to postpone the acceptance of an unwanted reality. This denial of all the indications that it must be a duck (quacks, walks, and looks) may provide a buffer to absorb some of the insult that would prove too devastating to withstand upon blunt impact (Kubler-Ross 1969). The body frequently numbs the senses and goes into a state of shock to avoid intense pain and tragedy. *The mind also seems capable of tolerating only so much before it needs to block some of the intensity of damaging perceptions and information. "Denial" is a common defense mechanism.*

Events most commonly met with denial include life threatening health issues, end of a relationship, and job loss. However, there comes a time when denial begins to interfere with the natural order of stages leading to a reality oriented acceptance of an unwanted life event. Coming out of denial often does not happen easily because of the dread of suffering through pain of seeing the disintegration of something highly valued. Once reality is no longer rose-colored by the lenses of denial, feelings of depression are likely to promulgate. However, this is a necessary evil as one travels the road toward recovery. *Frequently, one must come to the brink of facing reality several times before finally reaching a point of acceptance.* Coming out of denial requires the shedding of a protective insulation. For some, acceptance comes with a great deal of resistance. The next poem helps to prepare one for the often daunting process of kick starting the healing process. The poem relates to the fear and incredulity of the unthinkable circumstance. It gives the person a sense of anticipation of what to expect as he or she undertakes coming to grips with an unwanted reality. It helps the afflicted person to take steps toward beginning the healing process.

Prescription: Read throughout the day as areas of denial are surfaced. Then, recite as needed as the tendency to retreat back into denial is experienced.

Denial

Here comes the scary part
Let me close my eyes
Too much horror
I can't accept that it's real
Things like this don't happen to me
Others yes, me no
If it were true
It would destroy the things I believe
It would make grieve
Let me keep the door shut...

Knock, knock
Who's there?
Reality!
Whose reality?
Not mine!!!

Am I in a daze?
Am I getting the truth twisted?
Ignoring reliable signs?
Numbing to avoid feeling?

Let me open my eyes
Validate the implications
One by one
My sense of reality gets in sync
I accept
Step one to recovery

7. Detoxification

There is a decided therapeutic benefit to forgiving a trans-gressor. *Forgiveness hastens and enhances feelings of well-ness during the recovery process.* Nonetheless, under adverse circumstances, compassion can be elusive. This is especially true when one is insulted, betrayed, abandoned, assaulted, disrespected or otherwise wronged. Here, high-road decisions and behavior do not always come easily. It is proportionately challenging as the degree of injury increases. The inclination toward vindictiveness and retaliation may loom quite large after mistreatment. If allowed to consume one's mind in excess; hatred, self absorption, generalized negativity, and other toxic-ities can ensue. These maladies reflect the scarring of unfor-giveness. The irony is that *unforgiving reactions to injury can actually increase and prolong suffering.* Indeed, retaliatory behaviors frequently worsen outcomes. Obsessing about and holding onto affliction is a drunkenness that can slowly poison a good disposition. As it has been reiterated throughout this work, continually ruminating about things that are a source of agony festers depression and intensifies its impact.

Behavioral science research data supports the utility of forgiving as a means of lowering manifest feelings of anxiety, depression, hostility, and anger (Mauger, Saxon, Hamill, & Pannell, 1996). For example, *people who join with others for the purpose of fostering forgiveness (such as reli-gious or victim's groups) heal more rapidly and resolutely. They also meet with greater success at overcoming feelings of revenge and discouragement. Those who turn to addictive behaviors to numb pain and suffering are better able to cease self-medicating methods of coping after embracing forgive-ness* (Wuthnow, 2000).

As mentioned in an earlier section, blows to self esteem increase vulnerability to depression. Often, the repeated offenses of others significant in our lives damage self esteem and hopefulness. Studies (Wuthnow, 2000) reveal that women who were sexually abused showed measurable improvements in elevating lowered self esteem and reducing hopelessness after overcoming barriers to forgiving offending parties. Forgiveness, then, serves to inoculate one from depression and its cohorts by encouraging better relatedness to perpetrators of past harms, and less identification with the role of victim.

Despite the research data and spiritual wisdom found in the Holy Bible and great books throughout the world, that underscore the importance of forgiveness as a detoxification remedy, many find it unthinkable. It appears that the propensity to forgive is a function of maturity. Research shows that as we age we demonstrate a greater capacity to forgive (Mullet, et al. 1998). Here, it assumed that the more mature one gets, the better he or she is able to find a perspective that allows for the "repackaging" of the offenses to make them forgivable. It is hoped that the information given here describing the multifaceted benefits of forgiveness will motivate those suffering an affliction by self or others to mature their perspective to embrace this concept and gravitate toward forgiveness behavior.

The following poem is written in the form of a riddle. If read separate from the introduction of its topic, one might not know what answers to the call of the things mentioned. However, it should come as no surprise that this quality of behavior is often difficult to achieve. The poem and the information mentioned above relating to its outstanding therapeutic effects should give incentive to strive to achieve it as an essential component of the healing process.

Prescription: Read this poem daily after suffering an affliction that is challenging to overcome. Its message may appear counter- intuitive; however, it speaks the wisdom of the ages and is supported by contemporary research in positive psychology.

A Riddle

It's an act of selflessness
An attribute of the highest order
A decision that defies the natural instinct
A showing of compassion
A prescription for healing
The end of a disconcerting process
The beginning of peace

Its need never stops begging
It unrings a bell that once sounded
Reverses a pattern of behavior adopted
An elixir that dissolves wrongs committed
Fertilizes the soil for new seeds to grow
Puts a relationship back into forward motion
Brings things full circle

What encompasses all of this?
Forgiveness
Forgiveness
Forgiveness

Behavioral Interventions:

1. Activity Scheduling

Many *depressed people report a diminished capacity to enjoy things that had previously been a source of pleasure*. As a consequence, they may spend less and less time seeking or taking advantage of opportunities to be active. In fact, there is a strong tendency to withdraw from activity, especially from interactions with others. This lack of social contact and isolation from sources of constructive stimulation is often quite debilitating. The vast majority of depressed people wrestle with feelings of low self worth, inadequacy, and pessimism. Often, the depressed person suffers defeat in the battle to feel good about oneself. Consequently, she does not avail herself to the demands of everyday activity that she believes may judge her unfavorably.

It is the feeling of overall diminished capacity and resource to overcome dreadfully displeasing circumstances or situations that limit productive functioning. The first step in addressing these errors in self- judgment is to negate the inference that one suggests to the other. *Carrying out day-to-day activities in a fairly competent manner, counter-argues the indictment that one is damaged to the point that he cannot accomplish anything well and challenges him to attempt more things that bring value or pleasure.*

Scheduling and completing activities establishes greater normalcy and readily suggests that the person doing the activity must also be okay. It is the evidencing of occurrences that refute the blanket, negative impressions of self that allows the depressed mind to let go of convictions that assert he or she does not have what it takes to bounce back into a life that thrives. *Accomplishing activities provides empirical evidence that one is not inadequate or helpless and reduces the number and credibility of debasing*

thoughts that populate a depressive episode (Beck, et al., 1979).

The following poem makes concise the utility of being active. It suggests therapeutic rationale for getting and staying busy with activities of daily living. This poem is meant to inspire active participation in ordinary planning and carrying out of a "to do" list throughout the course of the day.

Prescription: The poem is to be read in the mornings as a rally call to defy the gravitational pull of depression that suppresses any inclination to get up, going, and accomplishing on most days.

Activity: A Necessary Condition

As mold flourishes in dampness
Flowers wilt in the heat
All conditions require incubation
Depression festers during isolation

Thoughts that keep one bound to home
Surrender to insecurity and fear
Suggests the idea that one deserves to be alone
Confirm that things are as bad as they appear

As laughter and gloom are seldom in the same room
Mood closely follows the mind
An oxymoron difficult to assume
It's hard to be busy and depressed at the same time

Make a schedule that spans morning-evening hours
Avoid the four walls of negative obsession
Create a variety package that never sours
Activity is a necessary step to overcome depression

As one accomplishes schedules of doing
Personal satisfaction is the result of the day
No longer supports a case for boohooing
Negative self-talk simply has less to say

It defies ugly vignettes the past wrote
Distorted beliefs onto a mental slate
It's not that activity is depression's antidote
Activity suggests a wellness state

Attending to Activities of Daily Living

One of the hallmarks of depression is a loss of pleasure derived from things that were once sources of satisfaction (Beck, et. al., 1979). Feelings of ineptness usually limit the amount of activity attempted, resulting in decreased happiness. Pleasure is realized as a function of completed activities that give value and meaning.

Depressed people are generally discouraged from attempting productive activity because they do not have the energy, resolve, confidence, or feelings of self-efficacy. In addition, they may feel pessimistic because previously attempted activities have had poor outcomes. Symptomatic of depression is a decline in the ability to concentrate, remember, and maintain the steadiness of tasks. Frequently, there are unrealistic expectations, impaired judgment, and lapses in motivation (APA, 2000). Activities that can be accomplished with success may not come to mind or may seem inconsequential. This results in feelings of low self esteem and inadequacy.

When preoccupation with failures is present, there is a strong tendency to stop attempting alternative or new things due to enormous discouragement. Often, *the depressed person needs to be reminded, in particular, of the various activities that can be readily accomplished and that offer potential enjoyment. They appear obvious and ordinary to the non-depressed person, but almost always need to be presented to the depressed individual as suggestions and recommendations.* Friends, family, or persons in the helping professions can be very instrumental in helping the depressed person identify activities that will provide a sense of worth and normalcy.

The depressed person must be encouraged to seek pleasure through purposeful activity. Here lies the first step in establishing a new sense of hope and optimism. "There are things that I can do that spice up my world and make me feel good about myself." The depressed person may need the actual assistance of others to help identify and select those activities most likely to be readily accomplished and offer pleasure consistent with what is deemed of value. The depressed person may have to be prompted to ask others to assist him or her in deciding upon activities that will be both doable and pleasurable (Lujuez, Hopko, & Hopko, 2001).

The next poem encourages activity that is essential to adaptive functioning in everyday life. It emphasizes spiritual, intellectual, and physical practices and concerns. It establishes a hopefulness that one can begin to take baby steps to get back to a pre-morbid state.

Prescription: This poem is to be read daily once a commitment is made to begin a regimen of therapeutic activity. This poem should be read daily for the first three months of therapy. It should be continually referred to throughout the course of a year.

Can I?

Say a prayer as the morning rises
Whisper another during the evening hours
Find a few moments of reprieve every day
Turn these moments into longer periods of time
Get out into the open air everyday
Go further soon
Play with my dog when his tail wags
Groom and care for my pet as needed
Admire something beautiful in nature once a day
See more to admire as the days multiply
Water my plants and flowers
Watch them as they blossom and grow
Read a few lines of inspiration early in the day
Affirm these uplifting words as the day progresses

Take a walk for part of an hour
More during the coming weeks
Start a small project that is awaiting my attention
Work toward its completion little by little
Do one thing daily to improve my appearance
With time, expand this into achieving other healthy
*   behaviors*
Think about something to change or add to my
*   home this month*
Less clutter, more comfort as the year goes on
Learn something new as I look around now
Use what I've learned to an advantage later
Realize an opportunity during the week
Follow up on its promise during the month
Pleasantly respond to greetings throughout the day
Have a little conversation before the day is through
Avail myself to play just briefly for a few
Longer and more frequently in due time

Get support from those that offer
Interact more as I know them better
Consider myself a few times a day
Experience more pleasure as time goes on
Save to treat myself to something special
Wow myself when the time is opportune
Love myself and others as love permits

Can I?

Very likely

2. Exercise Activity

In the previous section, the benefits of various forms of activity were discussed in relation to distracting attention away from thinking that promotes depression, as well as facilitating a sense of self-efficacy where the depressed person accomplishes things throughout the day that makes life seem productive and worthwhile. Exercise activity also accomplishes purposeful distraction and increased feelings of skills mastery. Additionally, exercise activity causes biochemical changes that improve mood. Studies (Johnsgard, 2004) indicate that *regular exercise 3–4 times a week, for 30–45 minutes significantly reduces depressive symptoms after a period of 2–3 months.* Persons who develop and maintain a regular exercise program show very impressive, sustained recovery from depressive symptoms.

Aerobic and anaerobic exercises show a similar result in improving mood. Medications, psychotherapy, and exercise activity are all shown to be effective treatment interventions.

Given the therapeutic effectiveness of exercise in treating depression, its inclusion in a treatment plan is highly recommended. The following poem encourages a regular program of aerobic and anaerobic exercise to assist in the recovery and maintenance processes.

Prescription: Memorize this poem. Recite it daily to encourage and prepare the mind for the therapeutic exercise regimen. The poem has increased therapeutic power if recited during the workout.

Getting Physical

My mood is lifted in increments
By daily, physical activity of 30 minutes
The weight of my problems pushed away from my
    chest
A great payoff for the time I invest
When I lack the motivation to get it done
I must force a brisk walk, jog, or run
Taking control of feelings of lethargy
By speaking spirit into a listless body
Bends and pulls, lunges and jumps
Cycling into gear out of the dumps
Arms, torso, legs, and thighs
Aerobic, anaerobic exercise
A treatment I give to my mind and my heart
The benefits are evidenced as soon as I start
The production of mood boosting endorphins
A preparation of self-made antidepressant medicines

Altruistic Activity

The more the depressed person is helped to realize that there are indeed purposeful activities that he can demonstrate ability to accomplish and derive pleasure from, the more likely he will be inclined to carry them out. Once completed, the depressed person can evaluate the benefit of these activities to determine how much inspiration they offer. After successive instances of positive outcomes and feelings of satisfaction are acknowledged, the convictions supporting pervasive gloom are seriously called into question (Lujuez, et. al., 2001).

There are many types of activity that can bring about increased feelings of enjoyment. However, the act of doing something for someone else is especially powerful in impacting mood. Altruistic activity addresses two things that support depression. First, it distracts attention away from the problems of the self and instead focuses attention onto the plights of others. Studies show that persons who sustain a dysphoric mood are inclined to focus their attention excessively on themselves and the sources of their dissatisfaction (Sloan, 2005). Secondly, altruistic activity provides a source of personal satisfaction and is a category of activity encouraged by behavioral approaches to the treatment of depression (Lujuez, et al., 2001). Huebner, Allen, Inman, Gust, and Turpin (1998) found that **altruistic activity plays a very important role in determining life satisfaction.** It is one of the components of the Quality of Life Rating Scale. Generally, the barrier to altruistic activities is initiative. Given that it provides a quick and robust return of positive self appraisal, and provides a means of positive distraction, **altruistic activity should be one of the first pursuits taken to ameliorate depressive feelings, once basic activities of daily living have been re-established.**

The following poem calls to attention the almost imme-diate therapeutic benefit of getting outside of oneself by volunteering to be of service to another.

Prescription: Recite this poem daily during the time of intense self absorption and self pity, usually common to the period just after the realization of a sorrowful life event. The poem is worded to show the benefits of and to encourage the active helping of others.

Altruistic Activity: A Quick Fix

How do you jump start the healing process?

Overcoming what keeps you depressed

Focus attention outside of self

Tap into a karmic wealth

Repeatedly revisiting the pot you wish to scour

Prompts you to realize the limitations of your power

Altruism affords a self healing distraction

A gift to others, a timely satisfaction

Be merciful to the ears of family and friends

*Positive exchange begins where self-absorption
    ends*

The merit of moving away from self-indulgence

Is a strong effort at moving into a future tense

When self focus only worsens the kick

Providing service to another provides a quick fix

3. Sleep Hygiene

Lack of sleep is highly associated with depression (APA, 2000). Changes in appetite and sleep are very common among depressed people. *Most often, depressed persons do not get sufficient deep and restful sleep.* There is a disruption of circadian rhythms caused by improperly regulated neurotransmitter substances, especially Serotonin (Thase & Howland, 2002). Although some depressed persons report symptoms of excessive sleep, those reporting severe depression more frequently endorse too little sleep, difficulty falling asleep, and waking up early or intermittently (Roesch, 2001; Zeuss, 1998). Most medical practitioners routinely target this aspect of biological functioning in treating depression pharmacologically. However, *sleep hygiene can also be very effective in ameliorating sleep problems.*

Sleep hygiene suggests that regularity of bed and awake times, reduction of caffeine, audio-visual stimulation and thought excitation, maintaining a sleep-conducive physical environment (cool temperature, comfortable pillows and mattress, elimination of distractions such as TV in the bedroom and extraneous sources of light, calming sounds such as white noise, ocean waves, or heart beat), and mind quieting activity such as prayer, meditation, and progressive relaxation can dramatically improve the quality of sleep.

The following poem addresses the relationship between depression and poor sleep. It encapsulates information that promotes good sleep hygiene. It summarizes and serves as a reminder of the essential components of good sleep behavior. Many suggest that good sleep hygiene practices should be implemented prior to or in addition to trying a short-term trial of sleep medications. Most prescribers agree that sleep-inducing agents should be used sparingly and for a short duration.

Prescription: Refer to this poem as a synopsis on sleep hygiene. Read to review behaviors and strategies that may be easily employed to improve sleep on a regular basis.

Rest

Need it to regulate the mood
To shift from emotion to thought
Gives mind to acquire the desires that elude
Life enhanced by the number of winks caught

Worry and lack of rest
A common bedfellow
Nightly, for those who are depressed
The head menaces the pillow

Sleepless nights, feelings of despair
One precipitates the other
Walls invite scan, ceilings a stare
Conspiring with one another

Too little sleep allows desperation to set in
Diminished access to Higher Power
Insufficient supply of Serotonin
Resilience does not flower

Circadian rhythms are offset
If sleep hygiene is poor
Delta sleep is hard to get
Many brain cells do not restore

Good practices help to hone it
Same time nightly sets the biological clock
Regularity of habit a key component
Pavlovian conditioning signals the sleep epoch

No alcohol, coffee or caffeinated drink
Four to six hours before turning in
No rigor, no fuss, no problems to think
Allows the shutting down process to begin

Clear the mind once in the sack
If awake after 20 minutes get out of bed
Warm milk, chamomile, a very light snack
TV and radio are practices to shed

A mindset that conjures dream delights
Concentrate on breathing or even counting sheep
A plan that promotes restful nights
Habits that induce snoozing without a peep

Positive Psychology Approaches

Prayer

Most people in America (86 percent) believe that God may be accessed for help with the problems we face through prayer (Dossey, 1997). One of the most common types of prayer is the petitionary prayer where one asks God for direction, inspiration, sustenance, courage, strength, and a host of other things that is lacking at any particular time. For example, during times of depression, one is most likely to feel helpless and in need of resources that are beyond what is readily available. Feelings of desperation may ensue. Many are propelled by their desperate feelings to petition God as a source of relief from indecision and anguish.

Frequently, the surrender to prayer is the end result of not finding sufficient remedy from self and professional help sources. Anecdotal evidence of this is documented by Douglas Bloch (2000). He writes about his personal experience with chronic depression that would not remit even after many trials of the most frequently prescribed antidepressant medications. However, after 90 days of concentrated prayer, supported by a team of 12, his condition completely remitted.

There is a growing body of research that supports the value of meditation and prayer in the healing of emotional and physical disorders. Dossey (1997) shares research indicating the efficacy of prayer as a sole or adjunctive intervention in the healing of various ailments and diseases. According to this research, both target-specific and non-directed prayers have beneficial effects including complete remission of symptoms and suffering. Non-directed prayer asks for God's beneficence to prevail in a particular situation.

This research suggests that non-directed prayer is more efficacious than stipulating a desired outcome. This is consistent with the instruction given by Jesus on how to pray (Luke 11:2-4). The non-directed type of prayer appears to have two to four times the potency over the directed prayer, notwithstanding the positive effects of both.

Of special importance in the treatment of depression is the prayer that represents surrender to God's will and timeframe in relieving the situations and circumstances perpetuating feelings of despair. This type of prayer combines a proactive approach to dealing with the malady as well as an acceptance of the supreme wisdom and power of God as is afforded by the non-directed prayer. The following poem expresses the mind and feelings of surrender after having exhausted all personal and local intelligence.

Prescription: This prayer is to be read or recited daily. It should be recited multiple times throughout the day when circumstances are bleak and personal resource is depleted. It is especially prescriptive for those contemplating giving up on life in a passive or active manner. It opens one up to the many and great possibilities that God can orchestrate.

My Supplication

Direct my way for I am lost
Strengthen me for I am weak
Rid me of the sick feeling that chokes my breath
  away
Encourage me for my supply of encouragement is
  low
Shoulder my weight for I am disgusted and tired
Provide a raft for me so that I may stay afloat
Restore my hopefulness with increments of
  responsiveness
Let the sun burst through a sky filled with clouds
Enlightenment me with the understanding of pain's
  purpose
Grant me the new beginning after the agony of the
  travail

Journaling

Journaling is a wonderful method of keeping track of change and progress. Journaling gives expression to feelings and behavioral reactions to daily events and passages of time. Journaling chronicles things deemed important and captures the emotional essence of occurrences that create positive and negative values. *Journaling provides introspection, an opportunity to look at what floats the boat.* Thus, *journaling is a great vehicle to chart progress.* By reading over the journals from previous days and weeks, one can readily see the benefit of the work being done to diminish depressive feelings. *Recognizing incremental progress is essential to the rebuilding of self esteem lost during a downward spiral.* Every day brings about learning and building of emotional fortitude. This lessens the power of the adverse conditions, and shortens the stay of the depressive episode.

Studies reveal that *writing about dreadful events helps one objectify the experience and gain meaning from the occurrences.* Written expression of the development and culmination of an undesired circumstance may promote closure and improved health if it facilitates a more favorable repackaging of perspective and emphasizes the positive qualities of the survivor rather than the negative emotions of the victim (Niederhoffer & Pennebaker, 2005).

The next poem encourages one who suffers from depression to journal the details, thoughts, and feelings of a negative occurrence to give voice to pent-up emotion and to document change and progress in the process of regaining previously established higher levels of cognitive and affective functioning

Prescription: This next poem is a mantra that affirms that progress is being made in recognizable increments. It is to be read daily, every morning. Continue until the depressive episode is over. It encourages by bringing into focus the accomplishments afforded by inching toward a desired destination. It affirms a systematic building of personal qualities and strengths that prove effective in ameliorating depressive feelings.

One Day Stronger

Every 24 hours brings opportunity for growth
Intervals between heartaches a little longer
More deliberate in saying the oath
Each day, one day stronger

Noting the progress as the morning comes
The list of positives gets longer
Encouraged by increase of air in the lungs
Each day, one day stronger

Realizing the effectiveness of the tools
Seeing the daylight longer
Decrease in self-imposed ridicules
Each day, one day stronger

Inching closer to accomplishing my goal
Better at maintaining composure longer
Bringing emotional wailing under control
Each day, one day stronger

Knowing that I am healing
All day suffering, no longer
Encouraged by the way I'm feeling
Each day, one day stronger

Chapter Seven

Depression Inoculation Strategies

❦

Pathways to Reprogramming the Mind

Embracing the Experience

Depression is likely after the fog of denial is diminished (Kubler-Ross, 1969). Once the reality of pain, disappointment, and fear set in, the symptoms of depression may be overwhelming. It is only now that the psychologically distressed person can come to grips with what the challenges his or her journey entails. Initially, most succumb to the weightiness of the unwanted condition. The wish to escape from the clenches of the sorrowful circumstances dominates. However, when the depressed person realizes the pathway to overcoming the pervasive sadness and intense dreadfulness at the root of her troubles is difficult to achieve, but not impossible, she is able to start the process of recovery. She then begins to move forward to address the dilemma head on.

There appears to be a natural cycle of hills that lead toward decompensation and valleys that lead to restoration. We tend to catch colds several times a year. Although the cold initially knocks one off of his feet, it provides a condition that causes the immune system to alter and better fortify itself. After the cold, the body is reconstituted to thrive better against a similar viral or bacterial attack. Although no one generally seeks to come under the attack of adverse conditions, one's power of resiliency is never proven until an upset or setback occurs. The suggestion is that *people often advance beyond where they were after a sorrowful life event.* There is something about the human organism that gives it the capacity to rebound and become better after an insult. As much of an oxymoron as it seems, *there appears to be a value in suffering through adversity.*

The poem that follows solicits a sense of optimism in the midst of suffering. It calls up the soldier within to consider the future benefits that can be achieved by fighting through the adversity. It provides a solace during a time of severe distress.

Prescription: Read three times a day during the acceptance phase of a harsh, unwanted reality. Use medicinally to swab inflamed areas of the heart and mind.

The Value of Pain

It alerts one to the source of an injury
Helps one to realize vulnerability
Puts one into a self-care mode
Helps to prevent a future episode

Causes one to stop and think
Helps one to judge the distance to the brink
Motivates one to repair the damage done
Focuses the mind on a good solution

Lessons flow from hurt and sorrow
Fertile ground for wisdom to grow
As new life sprouts from the downpour of rain
An urgent impetus to evolve is the value of pain

Acceptance

Eventually, one arrives at a point of realization where they must accept that there are some situations that are sealed in fate. *Once the individual can assure herself that all reasonable efforts have been made, stones have been turned, strategies have been exhausted, the job then becomes accepting the challenges and new possibilities that the disenchanting conditions present.* Here, one avails himself to the notion that the universe continues to offer benign opportunities for life enhancement after a setback or loss.

The next creative work is a pocket poem that directs one toward acceptance of the storm that has visited and caused havoc. Its presumption is that once all indicated resources have been exploited, one must allow the universe to once again present itself as a benign place to live.

Prescription: Recite daily during that period immediately after coming out of denial and the beginning phase of acceptance of the challenge of life after an awful event.

?

Life's Puzzle

"To be or not to be?"
Is the question
Once you've done all you can do
"Que` sera` sera`"
Is the answer

Regaining one's Power

Acceptance is admitting a powerlessness to effect any change over the presiding situations. However, there are circumstances that allow or even calls for responsive action. In fact, failure to respond can torpedo a sense of wholeness (as in half a man or less than a woman) and deflate self esteem.

High self-esteem suggests an ability to stand up for oneself, to be appropriately assertive, and not let others define who he or she is. Those who esteem themselves highly maintain a fundamental sense of well-being whether in the company of affirming, positive reinforcement, or in situations blasting unjustifiable, unfavorable feedback from persons of significance. Of course, the later circumstance is a lot more challenging. These offenses require highly developed assertiveness skills that defend against and neutralize potential harm. It is becoming increasingly more essential that people train in becoming formidable in asserting a demand for respect and consideration. This is especially pronounced in Western culture where the one who comes out on top is frequently the more favored person, despite the tactics used (Hewitt, 2005). A lack of skill in being appropriately responsive when insulted, put in a one-down position, made a fool of, or otherwise treated with a lack of positive regard or equality plummets self-esteem into a basement status.

Persons who esteem themselves lowly are among those most vulnerable to depression. They frequently withdraw rather than assert and stand up for themselves. They frequently allow mistreatment from others to transpire without adequately asserting a demand for better consideration. It is not uncommon for them to tolerate abusive language and conditions that diminish self esteem, parity, and relative power. Often, their kindness is taken for weakness.

They avoid "courageous conversation." As they endeavor to keep the peace, they may bite their tongues and forego expressing their feelings of abhorrence. As a consequence, *they demonstrate codependency, an unhealthy indulgence of offending behavior to maintain their position with or connection to an idealized person or situation.* This acceptance of unflattering comments and often abusive behavior is prevalent across many types of relationships including those in the workplace, friendships; especially romantic, and marriage relationships.

The most common cause for allowing oneself to be placed at the unfortunate mercy of another is not having sufficient verbal competency to adequately defend against an assault. Suzette Elgin (2000) describes a lack of verbal skillfulness as the factor limiting appropriate responsiveness to negatively motivated opposition. Frequently, in disparate relationships, one person is made to feel small by another who badgers or berates in taking advantage of their position of relative power. These relationships include those with bosses, physicians, professors, family, or lovers who offend at the expense of the other's feelings.

Dr. Elgin suggests that any defensive response tends to accept the premise of the unfavorable affront and does not competently disengage or counterbalance the attack. *Help in developing increased self efficacy in these types of encounters is achieved through assertiveness training.* She states that it is essential to be able to cause the person(s) who perpetrates the attack to justify her suppositions in a way that is based on objective rather than subjective and judgmental inferences as a means of decreasing the likelihood of future assaults. Proficiency in the use of tools of assertiveness is achievable through training and practice.

Lopsided relationships provide some of the best examples of self esteem deficiency. It is typically a situation where one person inflicts their anger, selfishness, and entitlements on another without regard for the other person's sense of dignity and equality of personhood. In addition, the undervalued person does not effectively combat the hurtful predicament, and consequently accepts part or the entire put down as indefensible. It is the epitome of a situation where self care takes the back seat to maintaining the status quo, accepting whatever is dished out rather than chance the prospect of losing permanent or even temporary connection to the relationship. *When there is very little self care, self esteem is at its lowest* (Beattie, 1990). Extended periods of not addressing self in a relationship equation may engender self concepts of unworthiness and inadequacy, both suggestive of low self appraisal and conducive to depression. *Feelings of despair and indignation cannot be ameliorated until the insulted person can gain increased reciprocity and assert his or her right to have dignity, respect, and consideration equal to that of the relationship partner.*

The upcoming poem captures the essence of degradation experienced as a result of inconsiderate, abusive treatment. It allows for a venting of pent up anguish and anger. It instigates a resignation to assert courageous determination to take a stand against unwarranted behavior. It encourages taking back power that was allowed to slip away.

Prescription: Read this poem once daily during the phase one commits to becoming more assertive in response to offending verbal, emotional, and behavioral insults.

What Am I? Chopped Liver? (On Being Assertive)

Palatable but lacking the appeal of caviar
Gestures of positive regard but from afar
Little reciprocated to the perpetual giver
Tell me! What am I? Chopped liver?

Seldom chosen as if distasteful to chew
Am I the spoiler dish on the menu?
Not seen as lean and tender
Prime filet of good taste and splendor?

When it's my time, it's so ho hum
It lacks the sparkle, lacks the passion
It doesn't feel good not to be good enough
Limp like a pillow that's been patted fluff

Difficult to play dumb as you cast your riddle
You conduct the music as I play second fiddle
My issues get placed on the back burner
I take it cause you're the primary wage earner

Not very high on the totem pole
At your mercy, under your control
Disregard saps the ego, deflates self esteem
Humiliating to have to endure its daily routine

My acceptance of this insensitivity
Allowing myself to be relegated to a Plan B
Communicates a passive attitude
A going along with being undervalued

I can't let others define who I am
God is my maker and not any human
I can't let your needs always supplant mine
Give me respect and I will you in like kind

You cannot exploit your notions at my expense
I cannot be expected to straddle the fence
You show happiness when I agree and say yes
Caving in makes me feel weak and depressed

No longer can I tolerate my rights being denied
I must develop strength of character inside
I choose options where my needs are fulfilled
I take charge! I'm responsible for the life I build

Chapter Eight

Relapse Prevention

❦

U p to this point, I have talked about vulnerabilities, cognitive distortions, hypersensitivity, and other personal frailties that heighten the risk of and/or intensify the experience of depression. The next foci look at characteristics, dispositions, and behaviors that help prevent decompensation into the depths of depression. Here, there is an emphasis on recognizing the early warning signs of oncoming coping difficulties, mobilizing resources, and strengths to circumvent a debilitating episode of depression. It highlights thinking and behavior that lead to damage control and healing. In essence, this next section introduces a positive psychology to better insulate individuals from, if not prevent, the onslaught of depression.

One of the attributes that helps to insulate us from depression is the ability to be in control of ourselves. Much of the suffering from depression comes as a result of losing control of our abilities to move forward in pursuit of meaning and good quality of life, despite adversity. Indeed, *if we build increased capacity to steer the course of our lives toward accomplishment and satisfaction by increasing the ability to reconfigure goals commensurate with changes in circumstances, the manifest control will make the best of the prevailing conditions.* Therefore, a sense of positivity may be derived from a new promise that is uniquely born out of the dynamics of change.

Maintaining control of emotions does not mean that one does not become emotional. Rather, it suggests that one actively manages impulses and feelings that will create externalized or internalized negative emotions that are likely to manifest unwanted, detrimental results. Studies (Thompson, 2005) show that persons who are able to maintain control as defined above are better insulated from symptoms of depression. *It is often a loss of emotional control, especially unbridled anger that causes deterioration in mental functioning and impairs judgment and adaptability.* Many of the techniques taught in anger management and domestic violence training treatment programs target the development of personal control that allow one to experience strong displeasure without discharging reprehensible or injurious behaviors to self or others. These skills permit one to be effective at appropriately responding to or challenging affronts and disappointments while not losing the opportunity to take advantage of positive derivatives being offered. These opportunities include a development of greater empathy, patience, impulse control, and resourcefulness in maintaining productive communication.

Personal control involves directing one's behavior through positive self talk. These are the same techniques used to walk through a complicated procedure or series of tasks. Behavior is thereby guided by the instruction of an internal voice providing a step-by-step sequence of actions that improve chances for a desired outcome.

The next poem underscores the importance of strength of character and self control in responding to words and actions that are perceived as disrespectful, insulting, or otherwise wrongfully used. It urges the use of conciliatory relations to stunt the expression of forms of retaliation that produce aversive conditions. It suggests perspectives that promote positive interpersonal exchanges and instructs the use of techniques to avoid talk and behavior that is mean spirited, aggressive, and suggestive of lack of control. This poem should be referred to during times of contention, especially when intense feelings of anger arise.

Prescription: This poem encourages the use of tools that hold negative passions prone to ignite explosive incendiaries in check. Recite as needed to avoid reactions that lead to sorrowful outcomes.

Personal Control

Listens without judging
Uses humor to diffuse
Accepts defeat without grudging
Never quick to accuse

Looks to conciliate
Times out to hold the peace
Continues to communicate
Until hostilities cease

Shows lack of resentment
Attempts not to scowl
Thoughtfully expresses sentiment
Practices self control

Under tense and stormy conditions
Self-regulates and does not bellow
Inhibits aggression of one's own volition
When testy currents flow

Appreciates the sense and value
Of getting another's needs met
Words an apology to undue
Behavior of later regret

Embracing the Now

After a major stumbling block, there is a tendency to keep analyzing details of the setback. We are continually in a state of contemplation. Rearview vision becomes quite keen. We try to figure out what went wrong over and over again. Frequently, there can be an obsession with what could have been done differently. If one perpetually appraises him or herself poorly, there can be a net depressive effect. To circumvent this, one must work hard to avoid prolonged indulgence in self criticalness. If one can shift her focus onto changing perspectives and behaviors that are productive and amenable to change, she can readily achieve increased satisfaction with quality of life and significant deterrence away from the doldrums of depression.

As we learn from critical junctures, it becomes increasingly clear that *missed opportunities to take advantage of showing and sharing love, giving time, appreciating the simple, but special things substantially subtract from the robustness of a rich and rewarding life.* Conversely, time spent learning, fellowshipping, playing, traveling, and communicating provide insulation from the preoccupation with sorrows that can readily envelope the whole perspective of life, and can lead to sizeable regret and sadness. This theme is amazingly captured by the Cat Stevens song "Cats in the Cradle." *Making the time for things that are of value as far as human-to-human relatedness is concerned is much more important than most of us tend to recognize.* As a result, we could all better serve ourselves and each other by availing ourselves to appreciate opportunities for happiness and enjoyment that are simple and of the moment. As such, if we can commit ourselves to realizing invitations to be interactive with loved ones, family, friends, and community, we can lessen the number of times we will have to experience the dysphoric feelings of wishing to have done things no longer opportune.

The next poem suggests a novel practice for many of us. Conceptually, we understand that we should not put things off that we have opportunity to accomplish today. Unfortunately, we often apply it to things like work and self-centered pursuits, rather than to interpersonal exchanges. This next poem encourages a shifting of tenses where those things readily assigned to a future time are acted upon in the present.

Prescription: This poem should be used as a morning mantra that provides excitement for taking advantage of daily opportunities to realize positive person-to-person relations. Read or recite this poem most mornings to frame thinking that allows for the embracing of now with regards to day-to-day positive life experiences.

The Future is Now

Possibilities that exist now may not exist then
Nothing about the future is certain
Enjoy the benefits of today's harvest
Countless tomorrows may add up to less

Nestled faraway in a cove warm and snug
Is immediately realized by a spontaneous hug
Great expectations of fanciful bliss
Readily traded for friendship, kindness, a tender
   kiss

Daily is the allotment of time
Many windows of opportunity to maximize
Never again this combination of circumstances
A unique recipe for epicurean advances

Constantly appealing to a time yet to come
Banking on the dividends yet to sum
Intentions don't assure completion of a vow
Fulfill today's promise! The future is now

An Ounce of Prevention

As we embrace the now, it is important to keep mementos, pictures, and other keepsakes for future times when these significant episodes may be appreciated anew. These treasures serve as memorabilia of remarkable life stories. They provide anecdotal evidence of a positive quality of living. Often, they are far from monumental. However, they document personal history that grows in value as time goes by. In fact, some of the experiences deemed unremarkable may be later determined as quite pivotal in developing perspective, character, or substance. These tangible products of the past may provide an increased sense of personal meaning. Researchers (Baumeister, 1991) suggest that we all have a quest for a meaningful life. *The four basic types of need for personal meaning that the researchers cite are purpose, value, sense of efficacy, and self worth.*

As we collect memorable items for later appreciation, we indeed store up samples of personal history that describe the various types of meaning we were able to achieve across the span of lie. These special savings provide good examples of the significance of our lives. The storing of these savings pays handsome dividends and refutes the content that emerges during times of low self appraisal. People who are able to transform negative occurrences into epochs of significant growth receive a benefit that provides insulation from precipitous self-derogation and ensuing feelings of depression. Those who are able to glean increased meaning and fondness of thought from past life events, both positive and negative, are less prone to depression (Baumeister & Wilson, 1996; McAdams, 1996).

The following poem recommends that care be taken to prepare for rainy days by setting aside things that may at some later date represent a treasure chest of pleasant memories. The poem fosters behavior that facilitates prevention of depression by making available tangible evidence of pleasure, and good fortune experiences at a time when there is a need to contrast the current span of displeasure with a previous time of decided pleasure.

Prescription: This poem is useful during the recovery period when one is documenting the pleasures of each day to disprove notions that life lacks pleasure. Read this poem one to two times weekly to reinforce the inclination to cherish remarkable moments and events by placing them into a capsule for a later time.

Rainy Day Memories

Tuck them away
Save precious memories for a rainy day
Mementos, pictures, cards; from few to many
Let them accumulate to be sure to have plenty
Sort them: Love, laughter, exhilaration
They'll prove valuable in times of tribulation
As storms come, loved ones stumble and fall
Time to remember having a ball
Shut in, disappointed, feeling despair
Go to the scrapbook, keepsakes, souvenirs
Anticipate days going from bad to worse
And when the good times go in reverse
Pull out the memories marked "gay"
They're good for the soul on a rainy day.

Observing Warning Signs

In looking at both the development and prevention of depression, it is important to be mindful of subtle signs of potentially harmful tidal waves as they emerge. Early awareness of incoming whitewater is essential. It gives one the opportunity to surface preemptive perspectives and responses that effectively minimize the power of the assault. However, it is quite common during the primordial stages to be dazed and, thereby, susceptible to injury if one is mindless of developments that should signal alarm, but are instead deemed unremarkable. The consequences of allowing these developments to fester can be quite harmful.

We must continually remind ourselves to be aware of threats to well being as they emerge. This is best achieved by talking to ourselves about how to make sense of things as they occur. Of course, it is not always possible to deliberate on all incoming information, but it is important to avoid going day after day on automatic, ignoring indications of oncoming turbulence detected on the personal radar.

The amount of negative change that may develop if early culprits are allowed to go unchecked can grow exponentially and put one at serious risk for a massive build up of dismay and bewilderment in a very short period of time. This blatant denial of an unwanted reality may inhibit one from responding to an alert to shift gears, to think and act outside of the box that dictates our normal assessment of situations, and subsequently causes one to fail to respond appropriately to threats to mood integrity (Langer, 2005).

Critical occurrences (losing a job, marital discord, academic failure, financial problems, and interruption of living accommodations) are the kind of issues that should be addressed with early, deliberate responsiveness. Too frequently, denial of the implications of these major life events leads to increased emotional suffering because there is insufficient preemptive responding. However, reactive rather than proactive thinking and behaving generally prove counterproductive and tend to cause a worsening of the emotional toll. Indeed, more consideration should be given to the many possibilities and opportunities of promise that are presented by situations and conditions we deem unfortunate.

If one remains active in the evaluative process as the shape of things take form, he or she can look for options that may provide more favorable outcomes rather than bracing for head-on impact. Inactivity, indulgence indecisiveness, passivity, and negative reactivity in the midst of brewing trouble generally prove not to be very adaptive responses and often allow avoidable, unwanted outcomes to occur.

The next poem encourages a mindful approach to evaluating occurrences that suggest the need to intervene prior to the culmination of a sorrowful end result. It promotes looking for barometers that forecast in climate conditions. Importantly, it encourages a mindset of expecting dynamic change as we journey life's continuum and an appreciation for the various perspectives and behaviors available to determine the impact of the changes. Finally, it underscores the importance of maintaining a self-protective analysis and approach to circumstances that may have grave consequences.

Prescription: Read this poem at the beginning of the day to set the mind into an alert and thoughtful gear.

Drive Defensively (Sorrow Prevention)

Life is often a tumultuous ride
A journey where hopes and disappointments collide
  Always important to buckle up
To better survive the ill-fated mishap

Look both ways at the intersection
Life's crossroads increase vulnerability
Be alert to the need of a course correction
Strong emotion often clouds visibility

Steer clear of the obstacles that derail
Stay between the goal lines of the road
Hazardous conditions will likely prevail
Observe warning signs and what they forebode

Detours are different routes to a destination
Alternative and novel, a medley of twists and turns
Not the plan of first inclination
A way of adapting to existing concerns

Inhibit rage against those who menace
Maintain a distance that provides a safety zone
Tragedy is borne out of actions that are mindless
The life you save may be your own

Chapter Nine

The Power of Optimism

❧

As mentioned throughout, once depression sets in it can be very disabling. If there is insufficient resiliency, the condition may take the depressed person out of the mainstream of thought and away from the community of support that is always available from family, friends, or a local resource. *The resilient person shows an ability to recover from setbacks. She begins to seek information, guidance, inspiration, and assistance that help to promote optimism about the possibility of a better tomorrow.*

Optimism and hopefulness as opposed to pessimism and hopelessness foster behavior and mannerisms consistent with an expected well-being. *Pessimism tends to foster an acceptance of an ill fate and does not inspire a call to action to take positive measures to challenge the odds of a poor outcome. The optimistic disposition produces a proactive series of actions that increase the likelihood of a positive outcome.* Sustained pessimism coupled with feelings of inadequate self-efficacy propels momentum toward greater depression The net result is that persons prone toward pessimism are more likely to experience distress and despair, with greater severity than those who manage to maintain a sense of optimism (Carver & Scheier, 2005).

It is extremely important to work diligently toward developing an attitude of expecting positive outcomes as a result of deliberate, proactive thoughts and behavior. An optimistic mentality encourages expectancy of a positive outcome or resolution. Optimists press on despite adversity, whereas pessimists tend to withdraw, distract themselves with behaviors that may temporarily displace the unfavorable conditions, and frequently allow the ominous circumstances to later overwhelm them without resistance. Many pessimistic people find it very difficult to shift their ways of thinking and perceiving to a gear that readily accesses optimism. Indeed, they frequently find those channels closed that would even consider a more positive, optimistic point of view. Again, this allows depression to take greater reign as awful circumstances grow more weighty and discouraging.

It is unfortunate that some do not have sufficient knowledge of the availability of healing, support, and care within their reach. This is handicapping to the extent that even when a person is aware that a positive outcome is achievable the person will likely not take any action to better the unwanted condition because he or she lacks the resource to materialize it. A deterioration of personal integrity and coping ability is a common consequence of no intervening modalities of help. Therapy and counseling readily assist in helping to develop skills and perspectives that increase self-efficacy. Cognitive-behavioral therapies focus on challenging the permanency and gravity of distressful life events, emphasizing perspectives and evidence that suggest hopeful prospects and a corresponding expectation of future well being. In essence, psychotherapies encourage optimism. A spiritual path is, without a doubt, a compelling walk toward optimism.

Optimists cope more effectively with and adapt more readily to disturbing situations. Optimists accept the indications of events they cannot alter as opportunities for growth and resign themselves to accept the circumstances as an unavoidable fate that is a part of his or her journey toward self enhancement. For many, optimism is an expression of spiritual faith. This latter way of thinking is frequently associated with persons who incorporate their Higher Power into their information processing and understanding of life events. Bible readers often find solace in the story of Job. They are able to find comfort and reassurance through their belief in God's infinite wisdom, faithfulness, and ultimate deliverance. Their faith is a powerful agent and greatly insulates these "believers" from succumbing to depression as a result of their faith in a favorable outcome. This is the essence of optimism.

Again, positive psychology research (Pargament, 1997) shows evidence of good benefit from spiritual beliefs that encourage optimism and hopefulness. People who see their plight as in the purview of God and are fortified by the belief that He will respond to their prayers, make divine intervention, and heal their illnesses, show better adjustment and disposition in managing day-to-day illness related problems. Conversely, persons who distance themselves from spiritual concepts or assume a blaming or negative view of God fair more poorly in overcoming both psychological and physical disorders. (Fitchett, 1999).

The following poem is steeped in the research mentioned in this section indicating that those who are able to affirm words of optimism and faith are given an extra layer of insulation from the throws of depression during a crisis or woeful life event. The poem provides a refrain that may be affirmed for increased optimism and therapeutic benefit.

Prescription: Read this poem morning and night and affirm the title throughout the day to improve positive expectancy or optimism.

The Tide Will Turn

As the waves rush forward to overwhelm
Its punishing force creates a struggle at the helm
Relentless pounding of strife and grief
In time, will recede to give relief

Strong torrents of emotion run a designated course
Then the ebb flow will return them to their source
Steep and turbulent waters gaining momentum
A life raft is down the time continuum

Two bodies pulling in opposite directions
Producing surges of hurt and rejection
Currents are dynamic and grow in intensity
Then give way to a lesser density

Looking ahead with a heartfelt confidence
Believing a change in favor is about to commence
Acting in accord with healthy optimism
Expecting an outcome cast by hope's prism

The difficulty is in enduring the onslaught
Learning from the painful lessons taught
It's an exercise in Job's patience
For those who believe in His presence

The challenge is to have faith in Him that would
Work all things toward a good
Bending without breaking the primary concern
It's inevitable! The tide will turn

Hope So, Oh No!

Closely related to the mindset of optimism is the spirit of hopefulness. *Hopefulness spurs concerted effort to accomplish something of personal or societal meaning. Persons without hopefulness lack the vision and sense of self efficacy necessary to achieve benchmarks he or she deems vitally important.* On the contrary, hopelessness signals a frustration of not being able to attain criterion-based standards of success or achievement and readily leads to poor self concept and increases the likelihood of depression (Snyder et. al., 2005; Bandura, 1997). Hopelessness is a form of depression that procedurally mushrooms in proportion to the thwarting of goals perceived as essential to a meaningful quality of life.

Hopelessness and its corresponding experience of despondency can be lessened by stepwise planning that makes goals appear within reach. The problem is that when depression-prone persons experience a paucity of ideas that generate pathways to achieving desired outcomes, they tend to shut down and isolate rather than connecting with others who may help them think outside of their limited boxes. This avoidance of the help that may be afforded by others is a mistake that is addressed in the poem "Don't Brainstorm Alone."

Depressed persons are very disappointed with their circumstances, themselves, and their prospects for the future (Beck 1979). Those that maintain a hopeful perspective are less likely to be inundated with negative emotion as a result of stressful circumstances, more likely to esteem themselves worthy of good fortune, and are subsequently less prone to depression (Snyder, 1996). In addition, *those who possess hopefulness generate more proactive ideas to deal with and reframe stressors than those lacking hope.* Hopeful individuals are less likely to imagine awful outcomes than those lacking hopefulness. Hopefulness then, like optimism, provides insulation against full-blown depression.

Self-efficacy (believing that one can attain desired goals and outcomes) gives impetus to hopefulness. The theory supporting the importance of self-efficacy and the value of hope in meeting the challenges of life's problems states that one must have a blueprint (pathways) and corresponding strength of being (agency) to surface hopefulness (Snyder, Rand, & Sigmon, 2005). In practical terms, this means *hope is generated by the development of plans that once properly executed will bring about a desired goal.* Conversely, hopelessness is created by lack of capacity and vision to bring about desperately desired outcomes. The human spirit is encouraged by the game plan that says victory is achievable by the implementation of its steps. Believability in the intelligence or wisdom of the plan is needed to ignite the energy necessary to carry it out.

The next poem couches the theory of hope. It is also a mantra that is melodic and provides encouragement when spoken earnestly. On a deeper level, the poem challenges the reader to spend time and collaborative effort in developing plans to cope effectively with and overcome obstacles negating goal attainment.

Prescription: Read this poem each morning as one looks forward to the day. Recite the refrain throughout the day to inspire or encourage belief that a well-established plan provides a blueprint to achieve relief from suffering and a corresponding desired outcome.

My Plan Says I Can

The odds are not in my favor
A struggle is at hand
My resolve does not waiver
Because my plan says I can

Slowly I walk forward
Barefoot in the sand
It's taking forever to get there
But my plan says I can

I think about giving up
Time and time again
The thing that keeps me going
Is that my plan says I can

Spells it out and makes it plain
Looks at barriers in between the gain
Directs actions within a time span
Essential is the plan that says I can

Often I'm reminded
By the One who supports my stand
Believe in what is written
A plan that says you can

Sequel:

If you can see it
You can say it
If you can say it
You can display it
All it takes is a plan that says you can!

References

American Psychiatric Association (2000). *Diagnostic and statistical manual of mental disorders* (4th ed. text revised) Washington, DC.

Bandura, A. (1997). *Self-efficacy: The exercise of control.* New York: Freeman.

Baumeister, R.F. (1991) *Meanings of life.* New York: Guilford.

Baumeister, R.F. & Wilson, B. (1996). Life stories and the four needs of meaning. *Psychological Inquriry,7,* 322-325.

Baumeister, R.F. & Vohs, K.D. (2005). The pursuit of meaningfulness in life. In C.R. Snyer & S.J Lopez (Eds.), *Handbook of positive psychology* (pp.608-618). Oxford, England: Oxford University.

Beck, A.T, Rush, A.J., Shaw, B.F., & Emery, G. (1979). *Cognitive therapy of depression.* New York: Gillford.

Beattie, M. (1990). *The language of letting go.* MN: Hazelden.

Bloch, D. (2000). When going through hell don't stop!: A guide to overcoming anxiety and depression. Ohsweken, ON: Pallas Communications.

Booth R, Bartlett D, Bohnsack, J. (1992). An examination of the relationship between happiness, loneliness, and shyness in college students. *Journal of College Student Development*, 33,157-162.

Brown, G.W. & Harris, T.O. (1989). Depression. In G.W. Brown & T.O. Harris (Eds.), *Life events and illness (pp. 49-93)*. New York: Guillford.

Brown, G.W. & Moran, P.M. (1997). Single mothers, poverty and depression. *Psychological Medicine, 27, 21-33*.

Carr, D., Neese, R.M., Wortman, C.B. (2006). Spousal bereavement in late life. New York: Springer.

Carver, C.S., & Sheier, M.F. (2005). Optimism. In C.R. Snyer & S.J Lopez (Eds.), *Handbook of positive psychology (pp. 231- 243)*. Oxford, England: Oxford University.

Dossey, L. (1997). Healing words: the power of prayer and the practice of medicine. New York: Harper.

Elgin, Suzette (2000). The gentle art of verbal self-defense. New York: Prentice Hall.

Fitchett, G., Rybarczyk, B.D., DeMarco, G.A. & Nicholas, J.J. (1999). The role of religion in medical rehabilitation outcomes: A longitudinal study. *Rehabilitation Psychology*, 44, 1-22.

Freeman, A. & Reinecke, M.A. (1993). Cognitive therapy of suicidal behavior. New York: Springer.

Gibb, B.E., Zhu, L., Alloy, L.B., Abramson, L.Y. (2002). Attributional Styles and Academic Achievement in University Students: A Longitudinal Investigation. *Cognitive Therapy and Research,* 26 (3), 309-315.

Greenberger, D., & Padesky, C.A. (1995). Mind over mood. New York: Guillford.

Holmes, T, H , & Rahe, R. H. (1967). The social readjustment rating scale. *Journal of Psychosomatic Research, 11,* 213–218.

Gotlib, I.H. & Hammen, C.L. (2002). Introduction. In I.H. Gotlib & C.L. Hammen (Eds.) *Handbook of depression.* New York: Guilford.

Grissom, S. (1996). DivorceCare workbook. Wake Forest, NC: DivorceCare, Inc.

Huebner, R. A., Allen, J. B., Inman, T. H., Gust, T., & Turpin, S. G. (1998). Quality of life rating: Psychometric properties and theoretical comparisons. *Journal Rehabilitation Outcomes Measurement, 2 (5), 8-16.*

Hewitt, J.P. (2005) The Social construction of self-esteem. In C.R. Snyer & S.J Lopez (Eds.), *Handbook of positive psychology (pp.135-147).* Oxford, England: Oxford University.

Johnsgard, K. (2004). Conquering anxiety and depression. New York: Prometheus Books.

Krieger, N., Rowley, D. L., Herman, A. A., Avery, B., & Phillips, M. T. (1993). Racism, sexism, and social class: Implications for studies of health, disease, and well-being. *American Journal of Preventive Medicine, 9* (Suppl.), 82–122.

Kubler-Ross, Elisabeth. (1969). On death and dying. New York: Macmillan.

Langer, Ellen (2005) well-being: Mindfulness versus positive evaluation. In C.R. Snyer & S.J Lopez (Eds.), *Handbook of positive psychology (pp.214-230)*. Oxford, England: Oxford University.

Lazarus, R. S., & Folkman, S. (1984). *Stress, appraisal and coping*. New York: Springer.

Leftcourt, H.M. (2005). Humor. In C.R. Snyer & S.J Lopez (Eds.), *Handbook of positive psychology (pp.619-631)*. Oxford, England: Oxford University.

Luejuez, C.W., Hopko, D.R., Hopko, S.D. (2001). A brief behavioral activation treatment for depression. *Behavior Modification*, 25, 255-286.

McAdams, D.P. Personality, modernity, and the storied self: A contemporary framework for studying persons. *Psychological Inquiry, 7,* 295-321.

Mahoney, M.J. (2005). Constructivism and positive psychology. In C.R. Snyer & S.J Lopez (Eds.), *Handbook of positive psychology (pp.745-752)*.Oxford, England: Oxford University.

Mauger, P.A., Saxon, a., Hamill, C., & Pannell, M. (1996, March). *The relationship of forgiveness to interpersonal behavior.* Paper presented at the annual convention of the Southeastern Psychological Association, Norfolk, VA.

Mullet, E., Houdbine, A., Lamonier, S., &Girard, M. (1998). "Forgiveness:" Factor structure in a sample of young, middle-aged, and elderly adults. *European Psychologist, 3, 289-297.*

Nicderhoffer, K.G. & Pennebaker, J.W. (2005). Sharing one's story: On the benefits of writing or talking about emotional experience. In C.R. Snyer & S.J Lopez (Eds.), *Handbook of positive psychology (pp.584-587).* Oxford, England: Oxford University.

Pargament, K.I. (1997). The psychology of religion and coping: Theory, research, practice. New York: Guilford.

Rando, T. (1995). Grief and mourning: accommodating to loss. In Hannelore Wass and Robert Neimeyer eds., Dying: facing the facts, 3rd edition. Washington, DC: Taylor and Francis.

Roesch, R. (2001). Encyclopedia of depression. New York: Facts on file.

Sloan, D.M. (2005) It's all about me: Self-focused attention and depressed mood. *Cognitive Therapy and Research, 29, 279-288.*

Snyder, C.R., Rand, K.L., Sigmon, D.R. (2005). Hope theory: A member of the positive psychology family. In C.R. Snyer & S.J Lopez (Eds.), *Handbook of posi-*

tive psychology (pp.257-287).Oxford, England: Oxford University.

Snyder, C.R., Sympson, S.C., Ybasco, F.C., Borders, T.F., Babyak, M.A., & Higgins, R.L. (1996). Development and validation of the State Hope Scale. *Journal of Personality and Social Psychology*, 70, 321-335.

Stuart, R.J., Blecke, D., Renfrow, M. (2006). Cognitive therapy for depression. *American Family Physician*, 73, 83-86.

Thase, M.E., Jindal, R., & Holland, R.H. (2002). Biological aspects of depression. In I.H. Gotlib & C. L. Hammen (Eds.) *Handbook of depression (pp.192-218)*. NY: Guilford Press.

Thompson, S.C. (2005). The role of personal control in adaptive functioning. In C.R. Snyer & S.J Lopez (Eds.), *Handbook of positive psychology (pp.202-213)*. Oxford, England: Oxford University.

Wuthnow, R. (2000). How religious groups promote forgiving: A national study. *Journal for the Scientific Study of Religion, 36,* 124-137.

Zisook, S., & Shuchter, S. R. (1991). Depression through the first year after the death of a spouse. *American Journal of Psychiatry, 148*(10), 1346-1352.

Zuess, J. (1998). The wisdom of depression. New York: 1998.

Index

Acceptance, 77, 101, 106,
  129, 136, 138, 140, 159

Aerobic exercise, 119, 120

Altruistic activity, 121

Anaerobic exercise, 119,
  120

Assertiveness skills,
  140-142

Attribution Theory, 98

Attributions, 95

Automatic Thoughts, 89,
  101

Cats in the Cradle, 149

CBT, 81, 85, 88, 99

Clinical Depression, xii, 33,
  34, 36, 37, 39, 43, 52,
  59, 75

Cognitive- Behavioral
  Therapy, 37, 81, 83, 85,
  88, 95, 99

Cognitive Theory, 47

Cognitive Therapy, 98

Constructivism, 72

Core Beliefs, 73, 81, 88,
  101

Defaults, 79, 101

Denial, 62, 106, 108, 135,
  155

Depressogenic thinking, 101

Distorted Thoughts, 81, 98

Forgiveness, 109- 111,

God, 49, 76, 128, 129-130, 161

Grieving, 56, 59-60

Healing Arts Professions, 63

Higher Power, 126, 161

Hopefulness, 163- 164

Hopelessness, 51, 63, 91, 104, 110, 159, 164

Journaling, 72, 131

Loneliness 52, 54,186

Major Depressive Episode, 34, 36, 39

Medications, 37,124 128

Meditation, 58, 124, 128

Mourning, 59-61

Negative Schema, 101

Neurotransmitter substances, 124

Non-directed Prayers, 129

Optimism, xxix, 95, 159, 160, 161, 163

Pessimists, 160

Petitionary Prayer, 128

Prayer, 124,128, 129,

Quality of Life Rating Scale, 121

Reframe, 97, 105, 163

Reframing, 81

Self Deprecating thoughts, 88

Self-deprecation, 95

Self-talk, 73, 146

Self-efficacy, 115, 119,159, 160, 164

Self-esteem, 140 142

Serenity Prayer, 40, 48

Serotonin, 124, 126

Sleep Hygiene, 124, 126

Stages of Grieving, 56

Subclinical depression, 34

Suicidal Ideations, 61

Suicide, 36, 63, 64, 66

Target-specific Prayer, 128

Printed in the United States
137267LV00001B/108/P